Surviving the Night

An AIDS Memoir

Douglas Saylor

Table of Contents

Preface

In the mid 1980's I was in my 20's. I kept a journal as a new disease devastated our community: it seemed important to chronicle what was happening. My friends and I were living in a difficult decade; our experiences were similar to those of other gay men coming of age then. These stories are dedicated to those who aren't able to speak for themselves; their lives were cut short. Most of the first names and a few details are changed.   The order in which I present incidents and people is not necessarily chronological.

Many things have changed since those sad, uncertain years. Now there are medical treatments available and society has made progress in dealing with the stigma of the disease. Ten years after I wrote these short stories I edited them and added postscripts for the people who passed away.

The title is from Emily Dickinson. Her poetry, focused on introspection and death seemed written for the early AIDS era.   I was sure none of us would be left alive. One of Dickinson's poignant poems is especially appropriate:

Somehow myself survived the Night-
And entered with the Day- (...)

Henceforth I take my living place
As one commuted led-
A candidate for Morning Chance
But dated with the Dead. (ca. 1871)

Versions of some of these stories have previously appeared in the newsletter for Being Alive San Diego and the *More Light Update* of the Presbyterian Church, United States of America, in the mid-1990's. I owe a debt of gratitude to the editors of those newsletters, Dan O'Shea and James Anderson, respectively, for first publishing my work and encouraging me to write.

Mardi Gras

I drove from New Mexico to Louisiana in the winter. I left the brisk, snowy mountains for the flat expanses of Texas. By the time I reached Louisiana the climate changed: the dryness gave way to humidity. As I drove from the northern part of Louisiana towards Baton Rouge, the vegetation grew denser; even the air was different. Swamps and bayous gave off a damp, wet aroma. I was 24 and headed to grad school, beginning a new chapter of my young life. I was going to study French, and Louisiana was a good place for that: it has a rich francophone heritage.

The Southwest, where I grew up, is for iconoclasts. Westerners want to find their own path and live by their own rules. Louisiana is more traditional. Brashness is not appreciated, restraint is. I tried to fit in but it wasn't easy at first. A politically connected friend in Albuquerque gave me the number of a couple to stay with; they took me in while I looked for an apartment and registered for classes. Jack and Phil, who were my age and active in local politics, offered quintessential Southern hospitality. They gently instructed me on how things work in the South and introduced me to their friends.

The first weekend I was there, Jack and Phil took me to a party at a country parish hall. J.T., the priest who hosted the soiree, lived in a rambling Victorian manse next to an old church. There was a cemetery behind the house and it overlooked the levee of the wide Mississippi. The rooms were spacious with high ceilings; because of its closeness to the river the place had a humid, slightly musty smell.

The guests were polite and restrained; occasionally the tinkling of laughter could be heard above the muted conversation. Because Mardi Gras was on the horizon, that was the main topic of discussion. "They say you always meet someone at Mardi Gras," one man assured me when he found out I was new in town.

Most of the people at the party were from good Southern families. I was not, and that made me slightly suspect. Being from the West, I wasn't quite a "rude Yankee" but I wasn't one of them, either. I was an outsider. South Louisiana is French and

Catholic; I am from an interfaith Jewish and Protestant family.

The table was spread with Cajun and Creole delicacies. I stifled revulsion at the centerpiece, a pig's head stuffed with some kind of sausage. "It's head cheese," Jack explained. "I'm sure you'll like it." I chose more familiar fare and balanced my plate in one hand and a cup of coffee with chicory in the other. Moving around the room was awkward and my plate tumbled to the floor with a crash. It happened, of course, when there was a lull in the conversation. Later Jack explained that it's considered bad manners to walk around while you're eating.

Thanks to Jack and Phil, I had an entrée into Southern life that I wouldn't have had otherwise. I'll never forget their kindness. Several years later they told me they had no idea who the friend in Albuquerque was who had given me their number. They didn't remember meeting him. "But standing out there on the front porch you looked like a lost puppy dog," Jack confessed, "so of course we took you in."

Slowly I began making friends. I was excited, when, after just three months of living in Baton Rouge, I was invited to my first Mardi Gras ball.

I still remember it, all these years later. I anticipated the prospect. Visions of mint juleps, verandahs and hoop skirts clouded my mind. I had so many stereotypes about the South, and some of them were true. I'd noticed that Southerners are snappy dressers; Jack and Phil made sure I rented a tux for the ball.

Even in the glow of young adulthood, I had a hint of how precarious life is. In both Albuquerque and Baton Rouge, AIDS had begun to cast a long shadow. In those early years of the 1980's, though, I was still able to put it out of my mind. I focused on the fun, excitement and happiness of going to a dance.

The ball would be full of gentlemen of society. I wondered if I would meet my future love there and wondered what he would be like. In those years, I believed in love at first sight. After all, they say you always meet someone at Mardi Gras and I felt sure it would happen that very night.

I was young and inexperienced. I thought romance was like a dime store romance novel; if anyone told me otherwise, I wouldn't have believed it. Life isn't like *Gone with the Wind*, but I didn't know that then.

I knew that Darren, my escort, was not the man of my dreams. I'd met Darren at Jack and Phil's place the second night I was in town. Darren was kind, shy, gentle, and never gave me more than a chaste hug. He invited me to go along with him and another friend.

It was beginning to get dark that early spring evening before the ball, and I turned on the lights. The spell of my dreams was broken and I felt silly. I put on my tuxedo, left my tiny student apartment, and headed for Darren's.

A surprise waited for me when I arrived: the man joining us was none other than Robert Devore. I met Robert Devore about the same time I met Darren, but unlike the gentle Darren, Robert seemed slightly predatory. Maybe he was just awkward.

Robert had invited me to spend the weekend with him down in New Orleans early in February, weeks before the Mardi Gras. I wanted to see the French Quarter, where he had a lovely home, but he wanted romance. Both of us were frustrated and I drove back to Baton Rouge early.

A couple of weeks after that disappointing adventure, I answered an interesting personal ad in the local gay newspaper. This was long before the Internet. An urbane, sophisticated man was seeking a friend. I sent a long letter and a photograph.

I had to laugh four days later when I got a response. It was from none other than Robert Devore, who asked why I left his place so abruptly. Hadn't he indicated his interest? Robert was angry with me.

It was awkward seeing him again and spending the evening together. He was a grouch and said the ball was just "vanity fair," full of young fluffs. Darren was puzzled by Robert's bad mood and my silence, but I was determined to enjoy myself.

The theme for that year's ball was Egypt, and every scene bore some connection to the grandeur of the pyramids and the sphinx. The main entertainment wasn't dancing but a *tableau vivant,* a kind of drag show. Southerners love drag: even the straight balls have elaborate cross-dressing acts.

Sitting on the balcony, I had a bird's eye view of the whole thing. I was told that many of the costumes took a year to make, and the participants spent thousands of dollars in sequins and ostrich feathers. Some the dancers wore a dramatic headdress, rising several feet above their shoulders. If the men had nice bodies, their outfits usually displayed them.

The auditorium was packed with handsome, well-dressed men. I noticed a distinguished man with red hair. I asked my companions if they knew him.

"His name's Alberto and he's from Cuba," Darren told me.

"He's wearing a toupee," Robert Devore snarled.

After the *tableaux*, there was dancing. I was determined to meet the Cuban redhead, so I moved closer to him and caught his eye. I introduced myself and he spoke to me with a thick accent. I shifted to Spanish, which I'd studied in New Mexico. I asked him if he wanted to dance. I was caught up in the magic of the night, the fun of a ball. No one looks bad in a tuxedo.

Alberto was not handsome but he was striking. Tall, tanned, even in winter, he was chatty. We talked of travel and of life in the South. He loved Baton Rouge. Alberto was fluent in French as well as Spanish and introduced me to his Cajun friends. Some of them spoke French: there are older people in Baton Rouge who don't speak much English.

I came of age in the disco years, and that Mardi Gras ball was one of the first times I slow danced with a guy. It calmed my nervousness. Alberto had a broad, happy smile, and the diamond ring on his finger glistened in the dim light of the dance floor. Of course, back then I couldn't tell the difference between a diamond and a cubic zirconium. Finally it got late and Alberto offered to take me home. How could I refuse? You're supposed to leave with the one that brought you, but Darren said he didn't mind and Robert Devore was glad to be rid of me.

Alberto had a little sports car and we drove leisurely along the levee road bordering the Mississippi River, passing little towns and old plantations. The river road runs from Baton Rouge to New Orleans; one of my most vivid memories of the South is that river road on the levee. In the following years, I'd drive it many times.

Late in the night, Alberto and I talked less.

"There is something I must tell you," he said quietly.

I was intrigued. Was the car stolen? I wondered.

"It is about myself. I hope you will still be my friend." I was puzzled. What secret could he have that would jeopardize our new friendship?

We continued talking, and he occasionally referred to the secret which he could not tell me. My mind raced in all directions. Was he sick? I wondered. AIDS seemed remote, far-off, something that only happened to swingers.

"Is it about your health?" I asked.

Alberto smiled. "No, I am not diseased," he said in a thick accent. He sighed. "I am wearing a hair-piece." Well, I already knew that.

"That makes no difference to me," I said. "It's not your outside that matters it's who you are in the inside." Of course, now, I wonder. Maybe it *was* the external that impressed me most at the time.

Alberto smiled, obviously relieved. He slowed the car and we parked by the river, watching a barge pass.

"I like you," he said.

"I like you too," I said. "Maybe we could go out sometime."

"Yes, good," he said. He leaned over to kiss me, and the sun began to rise on the river.

I saw Alberto every now and then; he was a *maitre d'* at a great restaurant and sometimes brought me leftovers from the kitchen.

Over time, I found something missing with Alberto: he talked about himself and rarely asked about my life or my studies. He was nice enough but our acquaintance never developed into a real friendship. We gradually stopped seeing each other; I became closer to other friends and got involved in school.

I ran into Alberto at a party, six months later, and he stopped by my apartment afterwards, to talk about his new passion, horse-racing.

Alberto died just months after that last visit. Darren called me to tell me he was in the hospital. I did not go see him, I could not even call him. He would be all right, I thought. I wanted to tell Alberto that he was going to be fine, that he would get better, that this was not a death sentence. I wanted to implore him to survive the night, as if that was something that could be accomplished with will power.

I dreamed of him several times while he was in the hospital. In my dreams, I comforted him, I talked to him, I told him not to worry. But Alberto died in a few short weeks.

"He just seemed to give up," Darren said.

I regret never saying goodbye to Alberto. I am ashamed I didn't go to see him; I did not even cry for him. He deserved at least that--- a few tears in his honor. But I could not cry. The era of AIDS had begun. We entered a new land, a strange territory. Most gay men were afraid and often the outside world wanted nothing to do with us. We had to begin taking care of each other, we had to learn to become AIDS activists.

I wish Alberto had not given up. Sometimes I think that if only I had talked to him, if only I had been there for him, to encourage him--- but would my words have mattered? I wasn't wise and had no special insight. I was lucky, for whatever reason, staying relatively healthy.

I quickly lost the innocence of that spring ball. Why some lived and some died, no one knew. In that small Southern town, the epidemic had begun. I lost my dreams of mint juleps on the verandah and reluctantly traded them for doctor's visits and memorial services.

Paris

I love France; I've studied the language and culture since my childhood. I first went there as an exchange student in high school. In my young years, I romanticized France. Traveling overseas was a great adventure and Paris was far away from the Puritanism of America. I met interesting people and went to beautiful museums: it seemed like a magical place where anything was possible. France seemed like a bastion of freedom and it took me a while to see its unique problems.

In college I spent summers in Paris studying the language. In the mid 1980's, I went there to escape from thinking about the new disease that was ravaging our community. I met interesting people and ate great food, but walking the streets of Paris, I was occasionally overcome by a sense of solitude. I fought sadness and depression; I couldn't study all the time and in quiet moments between activities, I was lonely.

One summer morning, fighting melancholy, I decided to go where I always went when I was troubled, church. I didn't know where else to go. I was still trying to cling to organized religion, to find solace. All my life I had been religious and at times it gave me comfort. Other times, religion seemed to condemn me. During those years, I struggled with my beliefs.

The American church in Paris was a place to go and hear my native language spoken. What represents America more than a church? It was also a venue for meeting people. After the service I went to the vestibule for coffee. That Sunday, I noticed a distinctively dressed woman. Her clothes seemed a little too big, giving her a baggy look which was just starting to become popular. She wore no makeup, which was unusual for a woman in Paris, and her long hair was pulled severely back in a pony tail. She was smoking a brown cigarette. The woman came over and introduced herself.

"I'm Kate," she said in a low voice. We talked for some time, and she struck me as a bit homesick. The American church provided something familiar, a common thread for all of us overseas.

I invited Kate to stop at my hotel for lunch; it was not far. I often bought bread, wine and cheese at a grocery store and ate in my room or at a park. Kate told me she lived the same way. She had been in Paris for several years. The hotel clerk stared at me as I took her up to my room.

I spread bread and cheese on the table while Kate talked. Any American living in Paris has a story, and she did. After several glasses of wine, she took off her horn-rimmed glasses and stared out the window.

"Five years ago I was living in California," she began. "It was a good life. I had loved Beth for more than 10 years and we lived together near the beach." She paused.

"One of her college friends was coming to visit. She had not seen this gal in years. They wanted to talk, so I decided to leave them alone that evening-- they had a lot to catch up on. I went to the movies. I guess they went to bed around midnight; Beth's friend stayed in the guest room. It was a warm night and she left the window open." Kate sighed.

"I found them a couple of hours later, when I got home. Someone had crawled through the window, stabbed her to death, and then went to Beth's room and killed her, too."

I was silent. Kate looked away and I took a deep breath. She seemed unmoved by the story, as if she were hurt too deeply to feel any more pain. No doubt she had told her tale before.

"They never found out who did it."

I took her hand. So that is why she lived in Paris, to get away from the horror. I hoped she had.

She left my room, and I was deep in thought. I measured my paltry troubles and occasional loneliness against hers. I hope Kate found solace. I saw her several more times while I was in Paris, and while we didn't become close friends, we spent some time together. She introduced me to other lesbians in Paris. I didn't confide my health fears in Kate or her lesbian friends. In retrospect, that was a mistake. Some of the real unsung heroes of the AIDS crisis are lesbians. They don't get enough credit for all they did.

Kate's French was flawless. When I had questions about French slang, I asked her. Sometimes I went to the Jewish quarter for kosher food. That summer, the main synagogue in Paris was bombed. In the ghetto I heard a new word. When I was first called "*youpin*" I didn't know what it was. In the years to come, I was called that several times. I asked Kate what the word meant.

"That was an ugly thing for them to say," she said, looking at me appraisingly, perhaps seeing something in my ancestry she hadn't noticed before. "It means 'kike.'"

One reason I saw less of Kate and her friends was because I met someone at a café in Paris. Philippe was a psychologist with curly black hair, about 10 years older than me. We started talking and discovered we liked the same writers.

I let myself be carried away by romantic fantasies. Philippe and I would fall desperately in love, and I would move to Paris. That would solve all my problems, I thought. I was waiting to be "rescued," though I couldn't say from what or who. I didn't know yet that I didn't need rescuing, that I could make it on my own.

Philippe invited me to stop by his apartment one evening. When I arrived, he was playing the piano; that grand piano took up almost all of the dining room. It was a cool summer day but the window was open. Philippe called to me to come in. He was older than I'd first thought, maybe 40, with a soft voice and a sweet smile. He motioned for me to sit next to him on the piano. He nodded at me, and I turned the page. "Almost finished," he said, finishing a phrase of music.

He was playing a Bach chorale that sounded hauntingly familiar. It was church music. Those Bach chorales are the backbone of the Presbyterian hymnal: at least, all those sweet sad songs that I loved so much during Lent. The titles were in German but I recognized the melodies. When Philippe finished I turned the page for him. There was   a   duet   and   I   played   with   him.

I spent a magical afternoon with Philippe. We talked about music, books, and finally about the mind. He was a psychologist, after all, and had studied many years, even going to medical school. I told him about Kate and we both shuddered.

As day waned, Philippe talked about himself. He had just broken up with a man he had loved for 12 years. How glorious, I thought, to have loved for so long and how sad to have it end.

Philippe asked about my life and I told him about my studies. I described both New Mexico and Louisiana. "Albuquerque sounds beautiful," he said. "And you'll learn to like Baton Rouge, too." At that time, I wasn't sure about the South.

He fixed a big supper, and we ate at midnight--- late even by French standards. It was late, very late, when we stopped talking. I looked at my watch. I couldn't take the metro back to my hotel; it stops at 2:00 a.m.

"Stay here with me," Philippe offered.

His bed was hard and I couldn't sleep. I tossed and turned for hours. He sensed my discomfort and towards morning he put his arms around me, holding me tight in his arms. I fell asleep at once, feeling safe and warm.

I began visiting Philippe a few evenings a week. Being with him calmed my loneliness and anxiety. Once he wanted to kiss me and I turned away. He seemed to read my thoughts, probably sharing my worries about the new disease.

He smiled. "Well, I can still hold you," he said.

Our hours together were pleasurable. Because he was a psychologist we discussed the dreams we'd had the previous night and their possible meanings. At times I felt almost too happy, thinking that I had perhaps found a safe place, a harbor to shield me from the storm. I was looking for a knight in armor. My expectations were unrealistic: no one can save you from yourself. I was young and hadn't yet grown up.

"I really care about you," I said to Philippe one evening.

He put his hands over my lips, as if to silence me.

"It would not be wise for us to fall in love," he said. "We live thousands of miles apart."

Maybe he was right. I was inexperienced in love and not always sure of what I wanted.

Several days after this, I was sitting in a cafe, reading a newspaper. I looked up and saw a redheaded man staring at me. I smiled at him and returned to my newspaper. He came over and we began to talk; he told me he loved Americans. His name was

Jean and he taught computer training to students in high school. Jean was talkative and told me he was divorced, with two children. He was about Philippe's age but less gentle, more direct.

We spent the afternoon together talking. I had never met anyone quite like Jean. He was pushy and aggressive but brashly honest. I found myself telling Jean things I had never told anyone before. He believed in sharing complicated feelings, ugly impulses, speaking without mental censorship. Jean was a combination of confessor and pop psychologist. Philippe listened to people talk about their feelings all day long, it was his profession. No doubt it was the last thing he wanted to do in the evening.

That summer in Paris was a time of intense conversations. From Philippe I got intellectual stimulation and with Jean I explored my feelings. As the weeks went by I could have chosen a deeper friendship with either one. I liked them both but in the remaining months I had to choose where to spend my time. Philippe was going to Switzerland and Jean was headed south to the coast. Each man invited me to spend time with him.

Jean was the most insistent and his aggressiveness persuaded me. He said he wanted for us to be together--- always. Philippe said it was unwise for me to fall in love with him. I was intrigued by the fact that I could talk so freely with Jean. Baton Rouge and Albuquerque seemed very far away, rarely crossing my mind.

I visited Jean on the southern coast. We spent hours on the beach, lying in the sun. We cooked together and went out to restaurants and nightclubs. There were moments when it was like a happy dream. But it was not all unbroken innocence: sometimes Jean took honesty too far and was highly critical of me. We whispered our fears about illness and disease to each other, late at night, long after his children were in bed. Sometimes I felt sick, fighting fatigue and nausea.

That summer, Rock Hudson revealed he had AIDS. While the American president was too squeamish to even speak of the disease, the Pasteur Institute in Paris was working on a cure. The French discovered the cause of the disease, a virus, at the same time as American researchers and there was a lawsuit to determine who was first. The French and the Israelis were spending state funds on research while my own country seemed to do little.

Jean, too, complained of feeling unwell. He was losing weight although he ate more than I had ever seen anyone eat. But we buoyed ourselves with the assurance that illness could not affect either of us: we had both been careful.

We drove to Nice and Saint-Tropez. When there was nothing else to say, I would tell him stories. I made up romantic adventure tales about men finding true love. We were rarely silent.

The summer was nearing an end and Jean said he would come and visit me in America. He wanted us always to be together, he said once again. I returned to Paris the night before my plane took me back home. I called Philippe to say goodbye.

Philippe sounded sad to hear my voice. He told me to come over, that I must spend my last hours in France with him.

Philippe said he had expected me to call or write, to come up and see him. I had been so caught up with sunny days on the beach that I had not even called, though I'd promised I would.

"I love you," Philippe told me that night.

I reminded him what he'd said to me. "You said that we should not fall in love."

"I do love you," he said, "and I thought you loved me, too."

I said nothing. He held me close for the last time.

One of the hardest things to learn in life, I thought as I took the airplane home, is choosing who to stay with and who to let go of. We all want love. Why is it so hard to find? Why is it never in the place you expect? And in those young years of my life, I had so many unrealistic expectations clouding my judgment.

I wrote to Philippe several times but he never answered my letters. I wonder how different my life would be if I'd chosen to stay with him that summer. Maybe I would have found a love that lasted.

Jean called and said he could get me a job in France. I was busy with my studies and didn't want to leave America. I wasn't like Kate, the expatriate. There was nothing I needed to get away from.

After a long period of silence, Jean called me. I didn't recognize his voice at first. It was late at night and I knew something was wrong. He gave me an address in a Paris hospital where I could write to him. He asked me to tell him a story. My mind raced as I tried to think of something to say.

"Tell me a long, beautiful story," he pleaded. I could tell from his voice that he was dying. And I talked to him, late into the night, telling him the most beautiful story I could think of, one about lasting love. I never heard from him again.

Wayne

One Sunday afternoon I joined a group of friends playing volleyball in the park. It was a typical summer day in Albuquerque, my hometown in the desert, and a dramatic storm caused our game to come to end abruptly. We watched the thunderheads roll in and stayed outside as long as we could. When the rain and lightning hit, we went to one of our buddy's apartments, where we soaked in a hot tub, talking, laughing.

A newcomer to our group caught my eye. Wayne was tall and thin, just a couple of years older than me. He said that his grandmother was Italian, which accounted for his dark good looks. Wayne seemed sure of who he was and where he was headed. I liked him immediately.

Wayne had just moved to town and was starting a life for himself in New Mexico. I still remember his first words to me. "I guess everyone tells you you're cute," he said, dismissively.

"Some people do," I answered, "but I'd like to hear it from you."

Wayne smiled maddeningly, not committing. We exchanged telephone numbers, but I didn't think I'd hear from him. I was staying at my parents' house and went back home that evening, reflective.

I wasn't in town for long. I had just two weeks left of my summer vacation before returning to graduate school in Louisiana. I was preoccupied because I'd decided to use that time to get tested for the virus that they said causes AIDS. I had my blood drawn at the county health clinic the Friday before I met Wayne. I was fairly sure I hadn't been exposed to the terrible new illness. Still, I didn't tell anyone one I was taking the test--- I was too afraid.

The morning after meeting Wayne I got up early. I loved to jog when the sun was rising and the day was fresh and cool. It made me think of the Navajo I knew who ran along the mesas. Running was a release for me, a joy. It was when I did my deepest thinking. It usually filled me with serenity.

That morning my thoughts turned dark. Since late adolescence I occasionally battled bouts of sadness. There were bleak moments when I was filled with worry and the future seemed dark and ominous. People everywhere were talking about this new disease. It struck us down when we were young. There was no cure, nothing the doctors could do. But surely that disease didn't strike nice people like me. None of my friends had it. And we were all pretty sure it had not made its way into the remote desert city we called home.

I'd been sick in the summer of 1983, two years earlier, a month or so after I had first heard of AIDS. I missed a couple of weeks of work with high fever and a sore throat. The doctor blamed it on a bug that I must have picked up traveling in Mexico. But even after I got better I had swollen lymph glands on the back of my neck. My father noticed them one evening when he put his arm around me. I discovered I had them under my arms and in my groin as well.

I went back to the doctor. This time he asked me, "Have you ever had sex with another man?"

I nodded, and he said, "Welcome to the human race." He frowned.

That made me nervous. I told my best friend about it.

"Do you think I have AIDS?" I asked.

He smiled. "Only promiscuous men and drug users have AIDS. Besides, no one here in Albuquerque has it."

I told another friend, a clergyman at the university's student center. He gave me a hug, and said, "I don't care if you have AIDS or how it's transmitted." That hug was a brave act. It was about the same year poor little Ryan White was driven out of his home and thrown out of school because he had AIDS. Another family with AIDS had their home burned down.

I went to see a specialist about my swollen glands. He said, "You could have leukemia, lymphoma, or AIDS." The name of the illness had been changed from GRID, "Gay-Related Immune Deficiency," to "Acquired Immune Deficiency

Syndrome" because hemophiliacs and Haitians were also being struck with the disease.

I could hardly believe the doctor's words; I was only 22 years old. I was sure my youth protected me, that I was invincible. Besides, I hadn't experimented with drugs or been promiscuous. They did a biopsy to rule out cancer.

The specialist did not seem so alarmed in the follow-up visit. He said, "Gay men all over the country have swollen glands. It doesn't mean anything and has nothing to do with AIDS. We're calling it 'Gay men's lymphadenopathy.'"

"Well, am I contagious or anything?" I asked.

"Oh, no," he assured me. "It isn't likely that all the gay men with swollen glands have been exposed to AIDS. The incidence of disease can't be that high." There was no test for the disease in those days, and I managed to put the whole thing out of my mind.

Still, that earlier incident scared me. What if the doctor was wrong? What if I did have the disease? But it wasn't possible, I thought as I jogged along the foothills. The idea made me sick to my stomach and I stopped running and walked home. What would I do if I had the illness? If I had AIDS, no one would ever love me. And what about my family? My father was a respected clergyman in the community. But I told myself I could not possibly have HIV.

My thoughts returned to Wayne and I smiled. I decided to call him. We both had free time late that afternoon and he invited me to his apartment.

His home reflected his personality. It was masculine, right down to the set of weights. There was nothing frilly about Wayne. His furniture was simple and practical. He'd removed the doors to all the rooms and put up long strings of wooden beads: it was an unconventional touch.

"So what do you like?" he asked.

Uncertain, I replied, "What do you mean?"

"What do you like? Tell me something you really, really like. Oh, I'll start." He paused for a moment, sighed, and closed his eyes. "I like watching the sun set over the rocks in the west when I've just come in from a hard day of manual labor. I like fixing a good strong drink. I love Scotch." He smiled.

21

"I like," I began, "backrubs with hot oil, the smell of pinion incense. I like going to parties and meeting new people."

The "I like" game continued well into the evening. We were so absorbed we lost track of the time and stopped only to eat. Late in the night, probably early in the morning, he leaned forward to kiss me. Thinking about the damn AIDS test, I turned away.

He seemed to read my mind and said, "Oh well, I guess it isn't such a good idea to do that anyway. They don't really know what's safe and what isn't."

I didn't look him in the eye. Wayne reached over and took me by the hand, leading me through those clacking wooden beads to the bedroom. "It's not long till morning," he said. "We better try and get some sleep."

He held me close. I dozed off and on, preferring to stay awake and feel the warmth and protection of his embrace. He held me tenderly throughout the night. I felt comforted by the regular rhythm of his breathing, and matched him, breath for breath, until I fell asleep.

I told Wayne I was soon leaving Albuquerque and returning to the South. I did not have much time with him, and we both knew it. I wondered if it was wise to pursue any kind of friendship because of our limited time together. Wayne said, "The important thing is that we've come together. Anytime two people touch, it sends out good energy into the world. When you love, even if it's only a short time, you learn."

Wayne was fiercely independent. I came to his house another afternoon, complaining about something trivial.

"Listen, I'm angry," I said.

He answered, "If something upsets you, it's your fault. You have control over what you allow to irritate you." Wayne told me about being angry with his parents once. "'Mom' and 'Dad' are terms of respect. If my parents treat me like a human being, then they deserve those titles. Otherwise, I call them by their first names, like, 'Betty, when you can be a grown-up about this matter then we'll discuss it,' or 'Robert, when you act like a father I'll call you by that title.' Works wonders. Try it."

I never did use his technique, but he taught me something else: I learned to tell

22

people when they hurt me. Maybe I became too confrontational: sometimes it's best to let things slide. Wayne was always direct, honest, but never a jerk. He had a lot of friends and every time I visited him we were interrupted by someone calling him long distance.

There were so many things that I wanted to show him, so much beauty I longed for Wayne to see. New Mexico really *is* the Land of Enchantment, and Wayne was eager to discover it all. We decided to go camping during our remaining days together. I wanted to take Wayne to the most beautiful place I knew, a campground near Bandelier.

How often, on lonely, sleepless nights, I returned to those ancient ruins in my mind. High in the rose-colored mountains of the desert were beautiful places, the long lost dwellings of the Old Ones. The Old Ones inhabited the cliffs hundreds of years ago; their homes turned to dust when their culture vanished. Their lives left a gentle footprint: only stone and pottery shards remain. Dust to dust-- no grandiose ruins, just a faint trace, a whisper of the past. I went to that place in my dreams, that sacred, holy place, the home of the ancestors, according to present-day Pueblo Indians.

In some shallow cave high in a cliff, I imagined sleeping next to a warm fire. The cave entrance would be guarded by a black bear, keeping evil away. In my mind's eye, a medicine man would fly to me, painted with holy marks, soaring on eagle's feathers. With sacred, healing words, he'd carry me high above the canyon. We'd stare at the stars of the clear, crisp night, the swift river flowing below us. The holy man would take me to a *kiva* where we'd dance to the beating of a drum.

I wanted Wayne to know this place, so I took him camping there near those ruins, though I didn't tell him my dream. Night fell as he cooked supper on the outdoor grill. We were all alone in the mountains. We talked and watched the fire burn. He, too, was touched by the beauty of the place. That night, he held me close in the tent. Wayne and I shared a special connection. I'd never met anyone like him.

After that nearly perfect camping trip, I had to face reality. A return home brought a return to the clinic and my test results. The doctor entered the room where I waited, my heart beating quickly.

"I'm afraid I have some bad news for you," he said. "From a public health point of view, you are like a malaria-carrying mosquito."

I left the office in a daze, struck by the harsh words. Time was now a scarce commodity, something to be treasured. It seemed like my life had just begun and now I had a death sentence. I sat in my car for a long time after getting the news, looking at the mountains in the distance. I felt alone and lost in a strange new territory. Nothing would ever be the same.

I didn't tell Wayne. I hadn't endangered him so it seemed pointless. Those were anxious times and I wasn't sure how he would react. I probably wasn't giving Wayne enough credit. He was kind and would not have rejected me. He was too gentle for that. But I kept my secret, too afraid to talk about it.

I went to see a wise psychologist who had helped me a few years earlier when I'd struggled with coming out. I cried as I told him my news.

"Don't make any hasty decisions," he said. "This is not a death sentence. You must go on with your life." He was right, though I wasn't sure at the time.

I had one more day before leaving and spent the afternoon at my parents' home. My mother looked worried. "The doctor called for you." My eyes began to well up. My father returned from work at just that moment. I did not need to tell them, they guessed. They were loving and supportive, not judgmental like I'd been afraid they would be.

Sadly I said goodbye to Wayne. He was disappointed in himself for being too self-conscious to kiss me goodbye in public. He didn't ask me to stay with him and I didn't expect Wayne to accompany me. He had just left the South. I looked forward to immersing myself in my studies. I planned on carrying on as if nothing had changed, keeping my secret. I thought I was the only one in the world who had been exposed to AIDS.

Wayne and I remained close, getting to know each other better, talking for hours on the phone. He wrote me some great letters, which I keep stored in a little box in my bedroom. That winter he wrote telling of a new love in his life. I could not be hurt; I had no claim on him.

I saw Wayne at Christmas time: when I reached to hug him, I felt a lump on the back of his neck. It was like mine, only larger. I said nothing. He had difficulties: his relationship was sometimes tumultuous and he could not find a job that suited him.

I visited Wayne again that spring; he was tense and nervous. He told me he was not well. Months later, I got a letter from him, explaining that he had gotten very sick but was better. He had decided to move to San Francisco so he could receive specialized medical care. I cried when I got the news. The dark new world of AIDS had begun: not just for me, not just for Wayne. Dark times had fallen on all of us.

Wayne's letters and calls were beautiful, sometimes humorous. Once he wrote me and told me every AIDS joke he had ever heard. Most of them are dated now, like: "What's the worst thing about having AIDS? Trying to convince your parents you're Haitian." He worked hard on self-improvement, and went to workshops and therapists. Once he called me, very late at night. He had gone to a workshop to practice dying. I tried to understand his exercise.

Wayne imagined and rehearsed the experience of death. He worked through his emotions. First, he said goodbye to his youth and looks and imagined himself worsening physically. He said goodbye to his vigor, to his energy. Then he thought of all his possessions: his records, books, posters, photographs. He visualized them in the hands of his friends, being discarded or given to charity. He rehearsed leaving his friends. He parted with all of us.

Then he contemplated his last hour. What would he do in his final moments, he wondered. He decided to write letters, saying final farewells to his mother and his lover. Then he said goodbye to life itself. I am still impressed with his bravery. Who is strong enough to meet death head on like that? I wasn't then, I'm not now. Death is like the sun, the French say; you can't look at it too long.

Wayne had practiced his death and it had not been easy. He sounded shaken. I hope it helped him for what was to come. He became very ill and was in pain. He wasn't able to maintain his weight. He recognized that Bob, the man he had been with for several years, could not be there all the time for him. Bob was in good health, and worked hard at a job with a lot of overtime. Wayne became lonely, depressed by the rain in the Bay Area. He decided to move to San Diego. Bob wanted to go back to Albuquerque where his family was.

Wayne was outgoing and made friends easily. That must have made the move easier. He was still looking hard, searching for something. In his letters from that time period, he wrote of a stark "spiritlessness" that plagued him. He even went back to church a couple of times, but it left him cold. His parents divorced after 40 years of marriage. He said there was no longer a unit called "Mom and Dad" that he had tried to please all his life. There was no home for him to return to.

One cold and rainy Saturday morning in Baton Rouge, I got a call from his roommate. Wayne passed away a few days earlier. I'd asked her to call me collect when it happened. His father had come out to be with him. Wayne's dad was a high-ranking official in the military, he was an honorable man who loved his son and stood by him.

I could not fly out to the funeral in San Diego, I was enmeshed in my studies. One night, I gathered up all the things he had given me, everything that reminded me of him. I cried over those lifeless objects, my only connection with him.

I got a letter from his mother several months later. She said she had been going through his correspondence and found some letters I had sent to him. It touched me that he had kept them. She wrote, "Like you, I loved Wayne so much."

Every now and then I think about camping with Wayne in the clear New Mexico desert. I remember holding him, talking and sharing. I remember other times I visited him in Albuquerque or San Diego. Sometimes, in crowded places, I think I see his face and want to call out to him, to touch him. I know that I can't. Seeing someone who looks like Wayne brings his memory to mind. All these years later, I still get lost in sadness when I see a tall Italian with a Roman nose. I miss Wayne, I always will.

Life isn't fair; and, as Wayne once said, the hardest thing about life is that you have to keep re-learning that lesson. It isn't right that Wayne's life was cut short. Why was I spared his fate? It's a question I continue to ask.

Wayne was right about something else: any time two people come together, any time new friends meet and love the world is a better place. They become better people.

I thought I was going to have Wayne for only a couple of weeks: we ended up having years together.

At times, in my darker hours when I'm alone, I feel his strength. If only Wayne were here, I think. He would know what to do. I wonder if he would have been the one I could have shared my life with. We always managed to be in sync with each other's moods. Even when I visited him in California we always struck a rhythm, a balance.

Wayne has remained with me, part of me, all my life. By some fluke of nature, I have outlived him; by a quirk of fate I ended up in San Diego. With the gift of a longer life, I feel the obligation, a happy one, to keep the memories of Wayne alive in me-- until I, too, become a part of someone else's memory.

The Birthday Boy

It was my 25th birthday and I was depressed. I got up in the morning and looked around my little student apartment in Baton Rouge. It was the pits. I didn't even have a sofa--- just a few cushions on the floor. I was 25 years old and didn't even have a sofa. Friends my same age had already made their fortunes. One had become a fashion model, another owned a couple of houses. I didn't even have a sofa.

My dumpy apartment was the least of my troubles. The summer before, I had tested HIV positive. Back in those early years of the epidemic, there was no treatment for AIDS; it was a death sentence. I saw the doctor every month and he always ended the exam by urging me to get my affairs in order, that there was nothing medical science could do. I felt alone and isolated, like I was the only person in the world with the illness. Because of the stigma surrounding the disease I told few people about my health.

Dating was difficult. Still, all wasn't lost. I phoned the man I'd started seeing, Elton, to confirm our supper plans. I'd met him at a party and we enjoyed spending time together. Elton had promised to take me out on my birthday.

"Hello, Elton," I said. "What time were we going out tonight?"

Elton was silent. "Did we have a date this evening?"

At first I thought he was teasing.

"I have to work late," he said. "Besides, some people from the office wanted to go for a drink."

I didn't remind him it was my birthday and that he had promised to take me out. I'd just gone out with him a couple of times; we weren't engaged. As I hung up the phone, I heaved a sigh of self-pity. I could suffer in silence. Twenty-five years old, without a sofa, without a boyfriend. I felt like a failure. Still, at least I liked graduate school. I didn't expect to be around a long time and saw no point in beginning a career.

Now, 25 years after my 25th birthday, and in the interest of accuracy, I am obligated to write that Elton was not a *schmuck*. He had a lot of class. He loved dining out in fine restaurants and frequently took me to New Orleans. The first time we went out, I reached for my wallet when the check arrived. "Why no, darlin'," Elton said. "You are a grad student and I'm a working professional. I don't expect you ever to pick up the tab. I just won't hear of it." Elton was kind; every student knows how tight funds are.

After a couple of weeks of spending time together, we parked in front of my forlorn student apartment building. Elton leaned over to kiss me. I had not discussed my health with him. Elton and I had friends in common and I assumed he knew; still, I needed to tell him myself. After my hesitation, he said, "I know there are things we need to talk about, but I like seeing you. I think you're cute."

Having AIDS made me feel ugly and undesirable; Elton's words surprised me. I didn't think I'd ever be wanted or loved. In the years since that time, God only knows how many times I've forgotten someone's birthday. Life gets busy and no one is perfect.

Later that afternoon, the phone rang. It was my friend Peggy. She and I met at a support group for family and friends of gays. She had just found out her daughter, Linda, was lesbian.

"Happy birthday," Peggy said. "I remember hearing you say that today was your special day."

"Thanks," I said.

"What are you going to do special?"

"Well, nothing really," I answered.

Peggy said, "I'm not doing anything later on. I'll take you out to happy hour to celebrate."

We agreed to a time and place. I met her at a dimly-lit Mexican restaurant at sunset.

"I thought this place would remind you of home," Peggy said. She knew I was homesick for New Mexico.

29

Peggy and I sipped Margaritas. She was a pretty blonde, which she said was not her natural color. Peggy dressed well and always had a smile on her face. She loved to laugh and had a Cajun zest for life. In Louisiana, the Cajuns say, *"Laissez les bons temps roulez,"* which means, "let the good times roll." Peggy liked cocktails and good food, which made her occasionally unhappy about her weight.

"Well, tell me about yourself," she said. "I know you've traveled and had a lot of adventures. Tell me about your boyfriends." She winked at me.

Peggy had been heart-broken when her daughter disclosed her sexual orientation. Her husband, William, had been even more upset. In time, Peggy had come to accept her daughter and was eager to learn everything she could about gays and lesbians. She attended all the lectures, support groups, every conference, much to the chagrin of William. Peggy told her friends and family in no uncertain terms that they were to accept her daughter's partner as a member of the family.

Peggy and I laughed, told jokes, and ordered another round of Margaritas. She giggled when I told her about my failed loves. *In margarita veritas.*

"Ooh, child, you have met some characters," she laughed. "I started out wanting to be a nun. I was in a convent for a while. That didn't last, I liked boys too much. I met William, fell in love, and got married. On the night of our honeymoon, of all times, I began to wonder if I'd made a mistake." She leaned in to whisper. "I remember thinking, I like doing this more than he does." She laughed, wryly. "That's how it's been ever since. He doesn't like to kiss or cuddle."

We talked and laughed together for hours, sharing secrets. I told her about Wayne and confided about my poor health. Very late, she looked at her watch.

"Well, I've got to go home and cook supper for his highness."

She hugged me warmly as we parted. "I'm sorry that boyfriend of yours stood you up. You deserve better."

It was a fun birthday, thanks to Peggy's kindness and sense of humor. I fell asleep happy, grateful to have made a new friend. In spite of the differences between us, we found common ground in our love of food, humor, and, of course, men.

Peggy and I started spending time together. She always spoke her mind and was in the process of becoming liberated. I'd never realized before how hard it is for women, that the same coercive forces that try to keep gay men down also trap them.

Peggy was making changes in her life. She gave up smoking, went to see a doctor about her weight, and decided to get a job so she could be more financially independent.

"William is just having a fit about all this," she told me. "He keeps telling me to stay home and to quit hanging around all those 'damn fags.' The last time he said that, I told him, 'for your information, your daughter happens to be one of those damn fags.' I slammed the door on my way out. He makes me so mad!"

I listened sympathetically as she told me about her husband. I often felt sorry for myself for being single but it was better than being in an unhappy relationship. I knew other middle-aged women economically trapped in unhappy marriages. They seemed to have no options.

Peggy and I went to parties together. Her husband would not go anywhere there were going to be gays or lesbians, so I took his place at those activities. New Orleans is a party city and Baton Rouge isn't far behind. There were always reasons to eat, drink, and get together with friends. And that wasn't even counting Mardi Gras.

Peggy was not universally liked in the community: she was outspoken and occasionally tactless. Like some of us with AIDS, she believed that her life experiences gave her the right to speak her mind. If you speak freely you have to be prepared to pay the costs; honesty comes with a price tag.

"You gays think it is so difficult for you to be yourselves," she once said to a group of our friends. "Well, let me tell you, it is hard for anyone to be who they are. It's hard being Peggy," she sighed. Those words have remained with me through the years. It's too easy to think you're the only persecuted minority in the world--- few people have an easy life. As my father always said, each of us is a minority of one.

Peggy was usually supportive about my health. Often she would go with me to the doctor and help me deal with bad news. In those days, that was all any of us heard. Doctors said that there was little hope. In addition, there was the shame and guilt associated with AIDS. I sometimes wished for cancer or some other disease with less social stigma.

Peggy's health was not always good. One night she called me from the hospital; I went right over. She was having severe diarrhea and running a high fever.

"Well, I knew that there was a certain amount of risk in being your friend," she said weakly.

"What do you mean?" I asked, surprised at what she was implying.

"They don't really know how it is spread," she went on.

When I went home, I worried, although I knew better. I called a friend of mine who had started the town's AIDS task force.

"Do you think I have given this to Peggy?" I asked.

He laughed. "Have you ever had sex with her?"

"Well of course not," I answered.

"Then you haven't given her anything. There are no cases of people giving AIDS to their friends without being intimate. If it was that contagious, everyone would be dying."

Peggy did not have AIDS; it was just a bad case of the flu. Neither of us ever mentioned the incident again. We continued to spend time together.

Peggy was great cook and loved preparing Cajun specialties. She made seafood gumbo, crawfish *etouffee*, jambalaya. Often she brought me food. One day, she decided to go against the edict of her husband, William, and invited me for supper. He did not want gays in the house--- least of all one with the AIDS virus.

"I don't care what he says," Peggy told me. "This is my house too. And you are so special." She hugged me. "I always wanted a son. And you are like the boy I never had."

Peggy treated me like a member of her family. When her youngest daughter got married, I was an usher in the wedding and sat next to Peggy on the front pew. It was an eye-opening experience for me. I had no idea weddings were such complicated affairs.

When Peggy met my mother, they talked at length.

"Your mom's trying," she assured me.

Minority sexual orientation is a difficult thing any mother to accept; too often they blame themselves. It sometimes takes parents a while to realize that no one chooses to be gay. Mothers want their children to be happy. They see the discrimination, persecution, condemnation, and stigma. The only real advantage is the possibility of doubling your wardrobe. And for that, you have to be careful to fall in love with someone who wears your same size.

Peggy and I went through a lot together. Doctor's visits, a couple of boyfriends, and the frustrations of life. The situation with her husband became increasingly difficult.

"I don't know what to do," she confided in me, teary. "The more I assert myself, the more he fights me. He wants me to be the way I was, and I can't be that anymore. That little girl has grown up." She sighed.

"I was 20 when I married William. Remember, I was raised a strict Catholic and planned on devoting my life to God." She stopped. "I think of all that bullshit I was raised with. I was so afraid back then. Why, anything you did, any thought you had put your soul in mortal danger. I was always afraid I was going to burn in hell."

I understood. I'd been raised in a religious household. As a child, I was frightened of the devil and hell. I suppose that is the whole point: some religious teachings serve to keep people afraid. Part of growing up is sorting out what beliefs and principles you keep and what you discard.

Peggy was crying. "I was a frightened little girl when I married William. At the convent, they told me I didn't have what it takes to be a nun. They told me to get married. So, I did." She took a breath.

"But the story doesn't end there. By the time I was your age, 25, I already had three daughters. I was ready to stop, but my priest told me I would go to hell if I used birth control. My health was never good, and one week I got very, very sick. I just didn't stop bleeding. They rushed me to the hospital and told me I had to have an emergency hysterectomy. Now, it was a Catholic hospital, and a priest was there. He told me I couldn't have a hysterectomy, that it would be a sin. I was still in child-bearing years, he warned, and he would not let the doctor operate. He said I had to have a special dispensation from the bishop to get a hysterectomy, and that would take weeks.

Now, picture this. That turkey is telling me I can't have a hysterectomy while I am literally bleeding to death on the hospital operating table. The doctor said I was going to die without that operation. The priest said he would pray for me, and anointed me. Well, William had had about enough by this time. He screamed at the priest and called him a bastard. Then he put me in the car, bandages and all, and took me to another hospital. Child, I was in there for weeks. The surgeon said I had already waited too long, and should have had the operation sooner. What could I say? But that's when I began to have my doubts about that whole religious trip."

She went on. "But it's still in me, don't you see? William treats me like dirt, and I can't leave him. In the back of my mind, I keep hearing what a sin divorce is."

"Maybe it's more of a sin to be unhappy," I offered.

"Are you turning into Oprah now?" she scowled.

About a month later, Peggy stopped by my apartment. I could tell she had been crying.

"I'm going to leave him," she said firmly. "I've made up my mind I can't stand this shit anymore." She told me the latest developments at home. It certainly seemed like grounds for divorce.

"Don't you have a lawyer friend, Harvey?" Peggy asked. We drove over to see Harvey and she filled out the preliminary papers for a divorce. As I took her out to supper that evening, she was crying.

"Don't look back," I said. "Don't have regrets."

Peggy sighed. "But I do," she told me. "I do have regrets. And what will I do? Go back to college? How will I live? How will I support myself?"

"Well, I do it," I offered. But Peggy did not understand how I could live in that little studio apartment of mine. When you're 50 and have raised three children, living like a student isn't much of a prospect. She took the divorce papers from Harvey and said she would look over them and get back to him.

A year passed. It was my birthday again and Peggy had a surprise party for me. The two of us no longer discussed William or the possibility of divorce. I did not want to push her.

We had champagne and it seemed to worsen her disposition.

She looked at me. "Child, you better enjoy these good times. You don't know how many more there will be."

My friend Harold looked startled, though everyone knew Peggy rarely minced words. "Peggy, this is his birthday," he protested.

Life hadn't been fair to Peggy. It's very human to take out your bitterness on those closest to you. We all do it. But I wasn't the source of her pain.

I stopped hearing from Peggy after that evening. She didn't return the messages I left on her answering machine. She dropped out of sight, no longer attending the parties or the meetings. She quit her job, took up smoking again, and started obeying her husband's rules. I happened to see Peggy, months later, at a department store. She'd put all of her weight back on. We spoke briefly; she was distant and cool.

Some might say that the fact our friendship seemed to end abruptly meant that we were never really friends. But that is not true. We cared for each other and that was what made it so painful. Peggy was trapped.

"We are all in prison, and sometimes the prisons are of our own making," a friend once told me. "The people that hurt the most are the ones who realize it."

Peggy knew she was capitulating; she knew she was imprisoned, economically and socially. I was learning that there were things just as bad as having AIDS. At the time, I thought Peggy was surrendering to her religious upbringing. Maybe it was resignation instead: Peggy accepted and came to terms with her fate, something that is never easy for any of us. It takes courage and grace to accept our lot in life. Just as there are costs to speaking the truth, there is a price to accepting that truth. The prize of resignation is peace of mind. I hope that's what Peggy found.

The Kiss

It was a beautiful spring Sunday morning in Baton Rouge and I got up early. Spring is the nicest time of the year in the South. The summer is too hot and humid; the winter is damp and rainy. In the spring, the azaleas and bougainvilleas bloom---it's glorious. That morning I decided to go to church. I had not been in a long time and there were friends I wanted to see. Even when I was angry at God, I occasionally went to church to visit friends and sing hymns. I had an ambivalent relationship with organized religion: many churches aren't kindly disposed towards gays, lesbians, and people with AIDS.

The service was in a luminous sanctuary made of wood and glass. On sunny mornings, you almost had to squint inside. The congregation was comprised mainly of gays and lesbians; it was near the university.

As the collection plate was being passed, I noticed a guy who was a couple of years younger than me. All through the service, my eyes kept wandering towards the dark-haired, well-dressed man. His shoulders were wide, and even sitting down you could tell he was tall and a little husky. His size would have made him intimidating but he had a friendly smile. After the service, when coffee was served, I went over and introduced myself.

Seeing him closer, I realized he was younger than I thought. His name was Harold and he told me that he was just starting college, making him around 19 or 20. I could not help staring at Harold while we talked, he was so handsome. He didn't seem to mind; he kept smiling shyly.

"I heard this church was liberal, and a good place to meet people," Harold said. His voice was deep and soft with a decided Southern twang. Harold was a big guy and would have been daunting if his voice was loud or too deep. His quiet tone made him seem like a gentle giant.

Harold introduced me to the woman he'd been sitting with. She shook my hand

and said, "Your face is familiar. Have I seen you on the news?"

"You might have," I answered. Several months earlier I had been on a local talk show speaking about gay rights and the experiences of people with AIDS. I saw no point in not speaking openly. I felt like my illness had given me the right to express myself. For one thing, I thought I would die very soon. In those years, I was learning to become an AIDS activist---we all were. President Reagan wouldn't even mention the disease our brothers were dying of. We felt alone, ostracized, and had to stand up for ourselves.

"Would you two like to join me for coffee and beignets later today?" I asked.

Harold nodded, still smiling in a friendly way. "I don't think my friend can, but I would love to."

We arranged a time to meet at the New Orleans-style coffee shop on the levee.

I spent the afternoon happily, looking forward to seeing Harold again. I felt the nervous anticipation that I often experienced when I met someone new. I hoped that this would be the "one," whatever that meant. My expectations were changing, but I was still looking for Mr. Right. I believed that everything would be different if I was in a relationship. I dreamt of a love that would conquer all, romance that was enduring and permanent, overcoming the ugly side of life. It took time for me to leave behind my childish Prince Charming fantasy.

Those first couple of years I was in Baton Rouge I felt lonely. My sense of isolation was compounded by my fear of telling people I had AIDS. I knew that any kind of romantic relationship would be difficult for me, nothing would be carefree or uncomplicated. Everything had changed in the age of AIDS. I was scared of rejection.

I was lucky enough to have found a gay "big brother." His name was Leon and he was wonderful. He wrote me long letters back in those years before e-mail. Leon surprised me with his unannounced visits about once a week. He lived in nearby New Orleans.

Leon was esoteric, with his own system of philosophy. He was gentle, sweet, and had studied for the priesthood before becoming a counselor. Ten years older than me, he gave good advice. Even so, I didn't risk telling him about my health, not at first.

I wasn't brave enough to disclose it; I was afraid to tell anyone.

Once, Leon asked me to describe my ideal lover. I said that he must be strong yet sensitive; attractive, wise and considerate. It was the usual schlock, but I was a true believer in Hollywood romance. Though this was decades before any discussion of gay marriage, I was looking for traditional matrimony. I didn't realize that what I wanted was as illusory for heterosexuals as for gays.

"Then you must be all that yourself. There is no knight on a white horse," Leon advised. "You must become the ideal lover you're looking for." Back then there were so few gay role models, I felt grateful that someone was honest with me. Back before "Will and Grace" or even Rock Hudson's death, the only gay guy people knew was Liberace, and his politics were disgusting.

All during that sunny spring afternoon, my thoughts kept going back to Harold. Even if he was not the man of my dreams, he could at least be a friend, an ally. Also, I had an obligation to help young gay men the way older gay guys had paved the way for me. I was impressed that Harold was sure of himself just starting college: it had taken me longer to come to terms with being gay. Maybe it was a sign times were changing.

It was twilight when I headed over to the New Orleans style café to meet Harold. I wore shorts and a T-shirt: he was dressed up and had a serious expression. His hair was perfect and he smelled like cologne. We sat down at a secluded table.

I've rarely been at a loss for words, but I wasn't sure how to begin a conversation with the earnest young man. I shouldn't have worried; Harold began to talk. He looked at me intently, his eyes pleading, looking for someone to understand. Harold needed to talk and it was a privilege to be there for him.

Though he was young, he had suffered. During the next couple of hours, I listened intently, barely saying a word. Harold needed that from me. His eyes welled with tears as he told me his best friend had killed himself. He paused for a moment, admitting that he had considered suicide when he became aware of his gay feelings. Before, during, and after AIDS, there will be gay teens who try to hurt themselves unless things change. Too many religious and political demagogues are happy to kick us around.

Harold told me about a beloved nephew who died. Once again his eyes were moist, and I took his hand, not saying anything. He stopped speaking and squeezed my hand so hard it was almost painful. It was an electric moment; I felt a chill down my spine. Harold looked at me, grateful to have found someone who listened without judging. It's what we all need.

This was Harold's night, he needed someone to care. By telling me the story of his life, he was giving me something precious. Talking about my problems would have taken away from him. Still, I wanted to make sure Harold knew about AIDS and how to protect himself when he chose to be sexual.

I took back my hand, hoping none of the bones were broken, and we fell silent. Finally, I suggested that we go for a walk along the levee of the nearby Mississippi. In the darkness, on the levee, we sat down. Once again, I took his hand. This time I held it carefully, mindful of his strength, and we sat close. Overhead, passing clouds occasionally blocked the moon's reflection on the wide river.

"Faggots!" an anonymous voice shrieked out of the darkness. We laughed.

"Damn," Harold said, "I thought it was too dark for anyone to see."

I put my arm on his broad shoulder, pulling him close, hugging him.

"You're the only man who has ever held me this way," Harold said. "Except, I guess, for my father, who used to hold me when I was a kid."

He put his head on my shoulder. Though he was much taller, it was not awkward; we somehow fit together.

After a few moments he said, "I've never been kissed by a man. I want to kiss you."

A voice within me cried "no!" I should have tried to stop him-- but he kissed me passionately.

Harold drew away, and took a deep breath. "That was nice," he said. "I have always wanted to kiss a man like that."

I said nothing. I continued to hold him close, a thousand thoughts racing through my mind. My life was on a different trajectory than Harold's. His life was beginning, and though there was just five years separating us, I worried that mine was ending. I felt guilty, unclean. But for that moment I continued the illusion, pretending that things were still the way they had been before AIDS. I remembered the first time I'd kissed a guy.

Harold returned home content and at peace. I spent a sleepless night thinking over what had happened, dreaming of a future that could never be.

Laurence

I was drinking a cool glass of iced tea with Harold's sister, Kathy, and her friend Regina. Iced tea is the quintessential Southern drink. People think it's the mint julep, but that's not true. The unofficial drink of the South is sweet iced tea. It was a warm spring day and the three of us were sitting on my front porch. The smell of magnolia flowers perfumed the air: the large tree by the front door had just blossomed.

I looked happily at Kathy and Regina. Both girls were young, just 18, and Regina's baby slept peacefully on my lap. The baby was 6 months old; I loved that child. Like ice tea, children having children is very Southern, too. Every few months the young women called and came over, always bringing the baby for me to hold.

By this time, Harold had found true love and moved away. Harold hadn't been single for long. Guys went for him like dogs to a bone, like white on rice. Why not? Harold was as sweet as he was good-looking; a real catch. Kathy and I missed him, and when she visited she often brought news of her brother.

"Did you know," Kathy said, smiling, between sips of tea, "that a man at work has been after me for two years?"

"You must be kidding," I replied. "Why doesn't he just give up? You're real cute, but you're not the only fish in the pond. Straight people are everywhere."

"Well, maybe he really, really loves her," Regina offered.

"I don't have that much persistence," I said. "I would not wait around two years for anyone. Not even for your gorgeous brother Harold."

"The guy is real religious," Kathy explained, "and he keeps telling me it is God's will for us to get married."

"God tells him this? Do you string him along?" I asked.

"I don't know," she answered, truthfully.

"He's a hunk," Regina said. "But he keeps telling Kathy how she's got to change her life; you know, she's got to stop smoking and drinking and foolin' around."

"I beg your pardon," Kathy said indignantly. "Just what do you mean by 'foolin' around?'"

"I think I know," I said. "You don't need to draw a picture."

"Anyway," Regina continued, "haven't you ever loved someone so much that you couldn't stand to be without them?"

I thought for a moment. "Not really. But I met someone who did."

"Who?" Kathy and Regina asked in unison.

"Well, there was this guy... his name was Laurence."

"Tell us about him."

"Well, Laurence was from here in the South, but he went out to Las Vegas."

"Why?" Regina asked. "To be a show-girl?"

"Sort of," I answered.

"Tell us the story of Laurence the show-girl," they begged.

I met Laurence when I had been in the South for a little over a year. One evening my neighbor from downstairs came up and suggested we have a night on the town. I reminded him that we were not down in the Big Easy, New Orleans, 60 miles to the south, but in Little Uptight, Baton Rouge, where there was only one gay bar.

"Oh, come on," he insisted. "You never know when you are going to meet Mr. Right."

It was Friday night and the little bar was jammed with people. As the evening went on, I noticed a handsome man sitting with a group of his friends. He was tall, I could tell, even though he was sitting down. He had soulful brown eyes and curly brown hair. He noticed my glances and smiled back.

After finishing my drink, I went over. I introduced myself and he was friendly enough, so we began to chat. He was in the advertising business, he explained, and asked if I had heard any of his commercials on the radio. I had. He asked what I did, and was unimpressed with my graduate studies in French. It was a common reaction.

"Why are you getting a doctorate in that?" he asked, as all yuppies did. "There's not much money teaching college."

I figured it was not worth my time to give him a sermon about the virtues of doing something you love as opposed to just making money. It was the 1980's, after all, and everyone had an M.B.A. and was going to be the next C.E.O. of Chrysler or something. I was swimming against the current, a free spirit living in the age of the yuppie. I liked teaching; besides, I figured I was going to die soon.

It was late and my eyes burned from the thick smoke in the bar. I suggested we go out for coffee. He agreed, and as we left, my downstairs neighbor winked at me.

Laurence was even more handsome in the bright light of the cafe and I was intimidated. Not only was I a poor grad student, but I was sick. Some gay men were afraid even to hug me.

"Tell me about your life," he said.

I plunged right in.

"I've had a little bad luck," I said. "My health is poor." It was better to say it up front and have him run away screaming than drop the bombshell after we had gone out a few times. It hurt less. You can't blame people for being frightened. Still, like little Ryan White said, if I wasn't infected I'd be scared too, but I wouldn't be so mean about it.

"Oh," he said, mildly. "That's not such a big deal."

I hadn't met anyone who told me that AIDS was not a big deal. This was 1986, and there was no treatment for the disease. Gay men all over the country, all over the world were dying. We spent our weekends going to funerals.

"I have had a lot of sorrow in my life," he went on, almost melodramatically.

"Tell me about it." Maybe it's ghoulish, but I'm always up for a sorrowful tale, especially if it's told well. Laurence was so good-looking he could have recited the periodical table of elements and I would have listened to every word.

"Well," he said, "I've just been back from Las Vegas a few months. My people are from here, of course." Laurence belonged to an influential Italian family. A number of Italians settled in New Orleans in the late 1700's, and some made their way north up the Mississippi River to Baton Rouge.

"I went out to Las Vegas because I wanted to get away from home and see the world. I lived here in Baton Rouge all my life and went to Catholic schools. I didn't have a college degree, and I'd never had to work, so at first I was just a dishwasher at a

43

casino. But I had a lucky break. I kept auditioning for singing and dancing parts. I always wanted to be an entertainer. Finally I got a job as a dancer at a club."

I didn't ask what kind of dancing in what kind of club. Laurence certainly had the looks for show business, as far as I could see. I would have liked to see more.

"I met a lot of people. Guys, and some girls, too-- would want to meet me after the show. I was never lonely. One night, a handsome, well-dressed man came backstage to see me. He said he had a jet waiting and he would take me to Paris that weekend if I wanted to." Laurence paused dramatically.

"I told him I had to work, but he said he had already talked to my boss about it. What could I say? It seemed like a great opportunity. I had never been to Paris before; he showed me the city in style. We stayed at George the Fifth Hotel and ate at all the best restaurants, even Maxim's. He wanted to buy me a new wardrobe but I couldn't have accepted that."

I wanted to protest that since he had already accepted the trip to Paris he might as well take the new clothes. But I kept my mouth shut.

"His name was Jack," and Laurence dropped a well-known last name. "His family has millions, of course."

I looked deeply into Laurence's eyes and wondered if he was telling me the truth. Had he really known that famous man?

"It was a bad idea, getting involved with Jack. I liked him a whole lot but I was not in love with him. I didn't love him the way he loved me." Laurence sighed. "I won't say I didn't have fun. It was like living in a dream world. He was always taking me somewhere exotic. I had never traveled before; Las Vegas was the farthest away from home I'd been. Things got very intense with Jack. He kept saying how much he loved me and that he could only be happy if I stayed with him. I told him I just wanted to be friends. But it was like an obsession for him."

While I wasn't completely sure I believed the tale, it was not hard to understand how someone could become infatuated with Laurence. Maybe he had made himself even more maddeningly desirable by rebuffing the millionaire's advances. There's nothing like rejection to stoke desire, especially for someone who's always had what he wanted.

"Jack used to send me expensive presents and eventually I just sent them back. He was trying to buy my love. I started dancing again and it made him furious. He couldn't stand it if anyone else looked at me." Laurence stopped talking for a second. He looked sad and I wondered if the story ended there. It didn't.

"One night, after the show, I brought a guy back with me to my dressing room. I didn't know that the janitor had already let Jack in. The janitor recognized Jack, of course. Everyone did-- everywhere we went. Maybe that was part of the problem. Anyway, this new guy came back with me, while Jack was sitting there, waiting for me in the dark. When the other guy kissed me, Jack lunged at him and started choking him. I didn't know what to do. I was stronger than Jack, but he was enraged. Finally, I pulled Jack off. The guy left in a hurry, saying he was going to sue Jack--- he had recognized him. I had really had it with Jack. I told him that his behavior was completely unacceptable, and that it would be best if we never saw each other again. I had been more than patient; I'd been willing to be his friend but could never be his lover. Now I didn't even want Jack's friendship."

I sipped my coffee. I could imagine a couple of guys fighting over Laurence. In addition to being handsome, he had an indefinable attractiveness, what the French would call "*je ne sais quoi.*"

"I left Jack standing there in my dressing room. He was sobbing. I had never seen him that emotional. But I didn't care. I was so angry. He had tried to control me and run my life; I was tired of it. It had stopped being fun and was turning into a hassle."

Laurence paused and sipped his coffee slowly. "The police came to my house early the next morning. Jack had hung himself that night and left a suicide note. He said that his life was empty without me, and that he could not stand to be alive if I didn't love him. Of course, his family was embarrassed about the whole thing and paid the press not to let the story leak out. No one even knew Jack was gay." Laurence became pensive.

I recalled reading something about the millionaire's mysterious death.

But it was very late and the coffee shop was closing. I invited Laurence to my apartment for more coffee.

I could see the look of dismay as he followed my car. I was not driving the latest sports model that he was. He was in for another shock when he saw my apartment. I was a student and lived simply. I didn't need fancy things.

"Well, at least all your money doesn't go for rent," Laurence said. Another friend had been kinder: knowing I was a student, he said, "It's good that you know how to live within your means. Not everyone can."

Laurence continued talking late into the night. He told me of the parties he had gone to, the celebrities he had met through Jack.

It was almost morning and I'd spent hours hearing about Laurence's glamorous life. I was sleepy. I was neither rich nor famous and my troubles were mundane. Thankfully, no one had ever killed himself over me. Laurence was good-looking, but surely there was more to Jack's death than a broken heart. If it hadn't been Laurence, it would have been someone, or something, else.

Laurence finally left without giving me his number or any way to contact him. I had listened to his story, and that was all he wanted. Maybe that's all any of us want--- someone to listen, a sympathetic, attentive ear. In those young years, I poured out my soul many times to different people. I owed karma.

The next day I thought about Laurence's glamorous life, comparing it with my own. Maybe my struggle with disease bored him. Living in Las Vegas and knowing entertainers, Laurence had probably seen many deaths due to AIDS. I couldn't decide if Laurence was superficial or if I was judgmental, jealous because I wasn't part of his well-heeled world. I'd never aspired to fame or fortune, more out of laziness than principle. At heart I've always been a hippie, a flower child. I was born 10 years too late.

A warm breeze blew and my attention returned to my young visitors. I poured another glass of ice tea for all of us.

"Was he telling you the truth?" Kathy asked. "Did he really know those people?"

"So young and yet so cynical," I said. I'd wondered the same thing; Laurence had no reason to lie unless he was pathological. I don't think he was trying to impress me, he didn't want anything from me, not even a hug goodbye. After listening to him for all those hours, it was the least he could have offered. I suspected much, maybe most, of what Laurence told me was true and I told the girls that.

As it turned out, I ran into Laurence a couple of years later. It was at a Christmas party, invitation only, for those of us who were ill. Back in the mid 1980's, a group of the infected came together periodically for social gatherings. It was an exclusive affair, kind of like belonging to the Junior League--- well, maybe not exactly.

I saw Laurence at this holiday party for the diseased. He had been drinking; everyone near New Orleans drinks-- especially at a party. And there was no reason for any of us to behave like Boy Scouts. Back then, you could just be a dying AIDS victim. People who didn't try to burn your house down felt sorry for you and maybe even brought you the occasional casserole. These days you have to be brave. You have to have a good attitude and be a long-term survivor, an activist, a hero. You have to work hard, stay healthy, think positive, and manage to keep all your T-cells in the process.

As I got ready to leave the party, Laurence came over to me, kissed me on the cheek, and said, "See you in the hospital, *cher*." "Cher" means "dear" in French, and the Cajuns pronounce it "shaw." Maybe Laurence did remember meeting me. I don't think he meant the words in a catty way. It wouldn't have hurt to have wished me a "happy holidays," but that's not everyone's style. Some folks can't muster Christmas cheer, even at a party, even when they're sloshed.

Laurence was a handsome man who had hung out with wealthy celebrities---at least, if his story was true. I'll never forget that night in a smoky barroom in Baton Rouge so many years ago. His tale lives on in my mind, casting ghostly shadows of lost love and lives that ended too soon.

Billy

I loved going home during December break. Christmas in New Mexico is beautiful: it's cold and crisp, especially at night, and the air is full of pinion smoke. The Sandia Mountains are usually dusted with snow. People put *luminarias*, candles in white sacks, along the sidewalks, so the Wise Men can find their way to the baby Jesus. The gently flickering flames bathe the December nights in gentle light.

I met Billy at a dance on Christmas Eve. I noticed him when I first entered the dance-hall. He was tall with a boyish face and curly blonde hair. He was staying with mutual friends who introduced us. Billy and I spent the rest of the evening dancing together, holding each other close for Christmas waltzes and *rancheras*.

I liked Billy immediately. He was smart, self-assured but not arrogant, friendly without being gregarious and honest without being tactless. He shared his feelings openly and invited others to do the same. About my age, Billy had kept the freshness without the naiveté of youth. He was so cheerful that his presence made others smile; he had the gift of making everyone around him comfortable. All of his good qualities were accentuated by his youthful, almost boyish bearing.

One afternoon just before New Year's, Billy told me about his life.

"I never knew my natural parents. They were both killed in an accident shortly after my birth. The couple who adopted me were wonderful. Very, very loving people. I loved them so much!"

Billy paused. "My mom, the only mother I knew, died when I was a teenager, and so it was up to my father to finish raising me. He did everything he could to spend quality time with me. He had to travel a lot with his job and often took me with him, especially in the summer. We went all over the country together."

He smiled, and then continued: "He was a liberated man. He had his little adventures, and I had mine. It never bothered him that I was gay. He said that if I was happy loving men, he was all for it. He had gay friends he introduced me to, and they took me under their wings. It was great."

Billy's face lost all expression for a moment. "I am an orphan twice, since he died. I have lost two sets of parents."

I felt sadness for him. But there was nothing tragic about Billy. He seemed even-tempered; the kind of man who could bounce back, strong, resilient, from any blow.

Billy had come to Albuquerque to see some friends. He had "burned out" on his job and was looking for a change. He had been working in the South and was ready to move back West where he was from.

"There's something about the desert," he said, "that calls me home."

Billy, like me, belonged in the West and was a little uncomfortable anywhere else. The desert landscape touched us both; it was the only place I could find peace at that time in my life. The desert is timeless: the blue, cloudless skies, the overwhelming luminosity and the dramatic mountains have always filled me with calm. Ancient cultures lived there for centuries, the Old Ones left faint traces of their peaceful pueblo way of life. I feel the continuity of nature in the desert. In the shadow of the cliffs and canyons, personal sorrow is temporary; even fear of death melts away.

Once, climbing a mountain path, I suddenly came upon a hidden meadow. If only I could die now, I remember thinking. I was overcome by the beauty of the field. Some people think the desert is desolate, but they don't see the subtle contrast of colors. The red earth, green meadows, brown mountains and silver forests change with each season. The desert teaches you to be observant.

Billy and I spent happy hours together, talking and hiking in the mountains. I was only going to be in town for a month and he had plans to move on, but that didn't matter. I was happy to have a buddy, someone to do things with. I told him about my poor health.

"I'm sorry to hear it," he sighed. "But that doesn't affect my friendship for you," he added, hugging me close.

It was a lovely moment. Billy held me like I longed for and needed. And as importantly, he listened.

At that time in my life, there was so much I wanted to say. I needed to air my fears. I was frightened and I didn't want to die. I was angry at the government's inaction and by some people's indifference. Billy listened, never judging, assuring me he understood. He held me when I talked, like I was the lost orphan.

One evening, at a dinner party, the subject of AIDS came up. Gay men were talking about little else, often in an accusative way.

"I'm sure I don't have it," someone said.

"It only affects people who are really promiscuous, or druggies," another guy added.

I was not strong enough to ignore that kind of talk: it cut me to the quick. I was afraid that no one would ever love me.

"I would certainly never go out with a man who had AIDS," the first man said. "I wouldn't even want him in my house. I mean, who knows how this virus is really transmitted?"

Then Billy interrupted: "You all are being so silly. They know that you can only get it through the exchange of bodily fluids. It just can't be transmitted any other way. And if you take precautions, there is no risk in even having sex with someone who has AIDS."

His friends fell silent, and we left the party shortly after. I was touched by what Billy did. He'd acted like a knight in armor.

"I hope you weren't bothered by what any of those guys were saying," Billy said as we drove home. "They're just ignorant and don't know what they're talking about. Just remember--- to people who really matter, your health status won't matter." He hugged me close. His comforting words have stayed with me all these years; he was right.

Billy held me in his arms for hours that night. We lay on a quilt before a dying fire, both of us safe from the world. The chill of the night drew us close. A log fell, and we both awoke from a deep sleep. The sun was just rising over the mountains.

"I love you," Billy whispered softly.

"I love you too," I said.

And I knew what the words meant. They were not a pledge of permanent affection or of commitment that would last a lifetime. But that made them no less precious. They were intense, emotional words. At that special moment, we shared love.

I returned to school in Baton Rouge days later, and Billy decided to move to the West Coast. In the following months, I got two letters from him. I have not heard from him since.

The French novelists write of "*les amours passagers,*" passing loves. But my love for Billy was more than that. He helped me to feel good about myself; he restored my dignity and made me feel less alone. I haven't stopped loving him all these years. I do not know where he is; I don't even know if he is alive. But this story is for you, Billy, wherever you are. Thank you for being there for me, thank you for that happy month in the desert. I love you.

Hurricane Parties and Healers

Bobbie did not look well on that cold, rainy fall day. I had never seen her so ill.
She was lying in a hospital bed at Holy Mother, a place she knew too well, and her face
was pale. Breast cancer, a mutual friend whispered to me. I never heard Bobbie utter
either word. Chemotherapy was to begin the next day.

Her lovely blonde hair was matted and her makeup was patchy. A pink lace
peignoir barely hid the bandages on her chest. Pink was Bobbie's favorite color; she
wore it frequently and normally it looked good on her. I entered the room awkwardly,
noticing her new friend Teddy by her bedside. She and Teddy had become close.

Teddy was perfect, I thought. He was tall, well-proportioned, handsome and
worldly. I envied and desired him at the same time. He was from a very good, very
old, very rich Southern family. Teddy intimidated me: not only was he good-looking,
but he was always calm, so serene. He believed in himself and in the power of his own
mind.

Teddy had spent thousands of dollars attending every mind-over-matter seminar
that I'd ever heard of. If self-help courses really did help, then Teddy should have been
perfect---which I suppose he almost was.   He read lots of metaphysical books and
assured us that he could heal his incurable condition, the illness he never named. On
rare occasions Teddy referred vaguely his "infection," as if AIDS was some irritating
trifle.

Teddy had been in the hospital a month earlier with pneumonia. He was very
sick, running a high fever. But he had not gone to the hospital, insisting that he could
heal himself by meditation. His father had finally driven up from New Orleans and
taken him to the clinic. His mother would not let him come home after that, afraid of
what the neighbors would say if they found out her son was gay.

The nurse brought in another chair so I could sit with Teddy in Bobbie's hospital
room. Bobbie smiled feebly and Teddy joked a bit. It was like a hurricane party. In

south Louisiana, when a hurricane blows, the safest place to be is in the bathroom. You fill the bathtub with ice and your friends and neighbors come over and drink hurricane cocktails until the storm is over. I found the concept of such a party problematic. In New Mexico, where I grew up, you wouldn't have a hurricane party. You'd have a support group and people would be in that bathroom sharing their emotions and "processing" their fears. And that was only right, I thought at the time. People should face the hard realities of life.

In the years since that hospital visit, I've mellowed. Back then I needed to verbalize everything. It's a family tendency; I was raised to speak my mind. I come from a long line of outspoken folks; in the 1930's there were meetings of the socialist party on the family farm. I've never been part of the mainstream and still don't know how to blend in.

Back in that hospital room, where all three of us faced hopeless medical conditions, I believed there was Denial with a capital "D" going on. I said nothing and for once kept my opinions to myself. Today, I don't know what I'd do. I suppose I'd probably tell a joke or say something mildly sarcastic, although there must be a middle ground, something between a cocktail party and psychoanalysis. I hope I find that balance someday.

Bobbie was Rick's mother. Rick was a close friend who'd died just months before his mother's cancer diagnosis. Rick knew everyone in town and kept me laughing with his wicked gossip. He had what they call a Southern sense of humor, which isn't that different from a Yiddish sensibility. Rick was always well-dressed, conscious of his appearance, like his mother. He called me every day at 4:30 p.m. We talked for 25 minutes, until the news came on or friends stopped by.

I met Rick the same place I met Teddy: the support group. There was only one in that small town and it was led by an open-minded nun at Holy Mother Hospital. Although we both got sick about the same time, Rick soon died. I outlived friends who became sick long after I did. I don't know how or why. It made me think of the Bible verse, "there will be two men sleeping in the same bed, one will be taken away, the other will be left behind" (Luke 17:34).

Rick always listened to my complaints, although he was much sicker. He understood the headaches, the nausea, the fevers and chills, and vowed to see that I was "fixed-up" before he died. His concern for my health was admirable. Even being so ill he took care of others. Rick and I used to go to the clinics together and try new doctors who might have something good to tell us. That was a rare occurrence back in the early years of the AIDS epidemic. One summer morning we waited hours to see some supposed guru specialist. He told us there was nothing to do but prepare for our deaths.

Rick never seemed depressed about his illness. He confessed that he had an uneasy moment or two, but he rarely ceased being graceful and witty. Once he told me it gave him a certain sense of power to know that he could clear an entire restaurant with one word.

Rick wasn't the first young man to experiment; he'd sometimes been a little wild. After his death, when his friends were together, we'd talk about what a colorful life Rick had led. I remember Bobbie confiding to me, "I don't want to hear any more stories   about   what   Rick   did."

One wet day Rick came over to visit. It can rain all day long for an entire week in the winter time. Southern rain is such a part of my memory I can still smell the dampness in my mind. The humidity permeated everything, your entire house and your very soul.

That wet afternoon Rick and I rented a scary movie. Horror seemed like an appropriate topic. Rick had become small, thin, frail: in a matter of months he was a shadow of his former self. I remember holding him close during a gruesome scene in the movie and thinking how little he had become. He was bigger than me when we first met.

Rick died two days after I came back from a study trip to France. I could not call him the evening I came home: I'd had such a wonderful time and felt so well that I wanted no reminder of the harsh realities of illness. The next morning, very early, a friend called and told me Rick was in the hospital. Two week earlier, he had checked himself into Holy Mother just like it was a hotel. He even told them which room he wanted. He had stayed in that room earlier in the year when he was in the hospital for a very long time. The room had a large window with a view of the garden: in the middle was a white statue of Mary surrounded by oleanders. Somehow they had the room ready for him.

Bobbie arranged for someone to sit with Rick most of the time he was in the hospital. She didn't want him to be alone and she was absolutely terrified he would die when it was just her in the room. Most of the time Joe was there; Joe was a big burly guy who looked like a truck driver.

The hospital called in a specialist who was squeamish about seeing AIDS patients. He wore a mask, gown and rubber gloves just to go in the room and ask Rick some questions. After the second visit of the "man in the space suit," as Rick called him, Rick dressed his large teddy bear in a mask and rubber gloves. The doctor got the point, and even learned to shake Rick's hand.

On that oppressively hot August afternoon, all of Rick's friends and family gathered in his hospital room. The room was full of beautiful flowers-- Rick loved them. If there were ever a week when his friends or family neglected their floral duties, he would call for a large bouquet to be delivered.

I didn't understand that all was lost for Rick; I was tired and wanted to go home. Out in the hallway, filled with the overflow of his friends, I said that I would leave shortly and come back the next day. Someone gave me a look I'll never forget, so I stayed. Rick gasped for breath for a few minutes before he died, a short death rattle. I had never been at anyone's deathbed before.

The week after he passed away I kept thinking, "I do not want him to be dead. I want Rick back." I said the words like a mantra, an incantation. Seven days after he died, I could not sleep. It was hot and muggy. I tossed, turned and cried for Rick until the early morning hours. Finally I left the bedroom and fell asleep on the living room floor next to the air-conditioner. I slept fitfully for an hour, finally rolling into something, someone. I cried out. Rick was standing next to me. I didn't see him clearly, his form quickly vanished, but I felt him as I rolled over. Rick was standing by me. I was startled more than scared.

I was afraid of seeing Rick's spirit again, scared of being haunted. What did Rick want? Some of my friends gently ridiculed my fear.

"You want him so badly to be with you, yet you know that he is dead. So your unconscious created the apparition," my friend Liz said.

Bobbie's daughter, Anne, and her son, the spitting image of his uncle Rick, were staying at Bobbie's house when Rick died. Bobbie called me the morning after my incident with Rick's ghost, reporting that Anne's son had gone into Rick's bedroom and run out screaming. The boy had seen Rick. For years afterwards, the nephew refused to go into Rick's room.

A week later I fell asleep in the afternoon. I had a vivid dream, almost a vision. I saw myself in a schoolroom. I was standing at the blackboard writing something. I stood back to look at the board and realized I had drawn a picture of Rick. Suddenly Rick was there with me. I took a seat at a desk facing him, sitting next to Bobbie, his mother.

Rick looked at her first. "You have learned about love," he told her. "You've learned the lessons of love you needed for this lifetime. You have made the supreme sacrifice of love. Soon you will join me and we will be together always."

Then he looked at me. "There is still a lot you have to learn about love. Ask my mother for help. She will guide you."

I woke up, crying, but at peace. I realized that Rick's apparition had come to me that hot August night to say goodbye. He wasn't there to frighten but to say the farewell he hadn't been able to when he was alive. I didn't tell Bobbie my dream, it was too personal.

After Rick died, I became increasingly close to both Bobbie and her daughter, Rick's sister, Anne. Anne had lived fast--- as fast as Rick. Anne was not well and wondered if she had been infected, too. I went to the health clinic with her as she took the test for the AIDS virus.

Anne did not have AIDS, but cancer. I stayed with Bobbie in the waiting room the day they operated on Anne. After the surgery, they told us it was very bad. Anne outlived her brother by only a short time. Rick's goal had been to live until age 30: he missed by a month. Anne died at 35. As I left the hospital the day of Anne's surgery, very late at night, another friend rushed through the doors of that women's hospital.

"I'm a grandmother," she beamed. "My daughter has just given birth to a beautiful, healthy baby boy. I'm on my way up to see them now." That moment of abrupt juxtaposition has stayed with me all these years.

Bobbie once brought in a faith healer to see Anne while she was in the hospital. He was from India and happened to be visiting the South.

"Before you go," Bobbie pleaded with the healer in the hospital room, "please work on my young friend. He has AIDS."

The Indian healer turned his dark eyes on me. He murmured a few words over the holy water he ritually splashed on his patients.

"Pray for God to forgive you," he said, "and you will be healed. God can do all things."

Pray for forgiveness for what? I wondered. For having an incurable illness? For being gay? I could have heard those words from a fundamentalist preacher of any faith.

The Indian guru was not the first healer I had tried. A year earlier my New Age friend, Lois, took me to see the Reverend Doctor Hal Paradise, a psychic healer with some renown in the South. Rev. Paradise and his plump wife, Doris, laid hands on me and visualized me well. Then they pulled on my legs to drain the bad energy.

"It has a rotten smell," Hal's wife Doris had said. "Same smell as cancer." She held her nose. I smelled nothing. Sixty dollars later, I felt no different.

Back in the mountains of New Mexico, my friend Emory introduced me to an Apache medicine man. One crisp, clear night in Albuquerque, my friends gathered in an old adobe house for a healing ritual. They stood in a circle around me, Emory beating a drum as the medicine man chanted. He burned incense and made me drink a bitter tea. I lay on the cool floor and felt emotional healing through the love and concern of my friends.

Back in those days we tried herbal remedies as well. There were various teas, Chinese cucumber, forms of lecithin. We had many false hopes as some Israeli or

French scientist would announce a cure. I kept my passport ready, prepared to travel overseas at any moment. It's easy to chuckle at the various cures and treatments we used, but, as with prayer, you can't prove they didn't have some effect.

There was a lot of New Age belief in those early days of the epidemic. The support group where I met Rick, and later, Teddy, was dripping with positive thought.

"I know that if I keep my thoughts positive and uplifting, I will not get sick. It is up to me to choose sickness or health," Teddy once said. "We chose this manifestation before we came to the earth plane," Teddy continued. "We chose everything about our lives." Teddy went on: "The Christian era is the age of suffering. In the New Age, people will no longer choose to learn through suffering."

I did not say anything, but it took effort not to roll my eyes. Catching a virus is a random thing. It has more to do with being at the wrong place at the wrong time than your frame of mind.

Once, my New Age friend, Lois, called to console me when I was grieving a friend's death.

"Just remember," Lois said, "He chose to die, he chose to have AIDS. He chose this manifestation, just like you." I hung up the phone on her.

Another time, Lois came over to align my *chakras*. I called Bobbie the next day to tell her about it.

"Excuse me," Bobbie said, in an offended tone. "I do not need to hear about your private life. Besides, I thought you were gay."

I explained that it was not some bizarre sexual act, but that Lois waved a crystal over me to align my energy fields.

"Oh," Bobbie said, unimpressed. "Well, I see people now wearing those rocks swinging around their necks. All I know is that when I was a girl and we couldn't afford diamonds, my mother and I both wore crystals. That was before God created the cubic zirconium." She giggled. "Don't you ever tell a soul, but that gold diamond pin on my fur coat is crystal. Everyone admires it and they all think it's real. I can't say I ever feel any healing energy when I wear it. On the other hand, I suppose it is magical when people think that something your grandmother bought at Kresge's came from Tiffany."

Bobbie's beliefs were more traditional, though she was willing to try anything to help cure her family and friends. She was a convert to Catholicism, explaining that as a child she was embarrassed by all the yelling and carrying on in the pulpit at the Baptist church. She thought the Catholic religion was beautiful and loved the pageantry of the mass. Her mother was horrified and promised her a full-length mink coat and a trip to Hawaii if she would reconsider. But Bobbie didn't. Often she would stand over Rick's hospital bed saying the rosary. It drove him crazy.

My beliefs were evolving during those years. Clinging to the Jewish and Presbyterian faiths of my childhood seemed out of style with all the metaphysical ideas going around. In fairness, traditional denominations didn't offer much comfort to those of us with AIDS. There were notable exceptions, of course, like Holy Mother Hospital.

A friend who fought depression came to the support group at Holy Mother that Teddy, Rick and I attended. He brought a letter he'd received. The understanding nun who counseled us asked him to read it.

"It's from a psychic," he told us. "She channels this energy called Elias." He softly read: "Gay people have a special place in the universal consciousness. They are not bad or sinful. They have a specific role in the world." His eyes filled with tears as he continued to read.

"AIDS should not be seen as any kind of punishment from the Divine. Higher souls have chosen this difficult pathway to help teach others compassion." He cried softly. "It is not a punishment from God."

We were all silent. Sister smiled. "I'm glad you have found something that has given you such comfort." I patted his shoulder as he choked back tears.

A month after Rick's death, Bobbie went to a psychic, the same one who channeled Elias. Channeling was a big deal in the 1980's, even in the South. Bobbie wanted desperately to talk to the son she missed so much. She also wanted to know if Rick was with his father, who had died in a car accident a couple of years earlier.

"Rick hasn't found his father yet," the psychic said. I wondered if it was just a ploy to get a return visit and make some more money. Bobbie never told me if she went back.

Bobbie had been through so much: the death of her husband at a young age, the deaths of both her son and daughter, and now a cancer diagnosis. Fortunately she was well-loved and had many friends.

"Bobbie has had bad luck," her friends Pete and Millie said. Millie's son also had AIDS, but he was like the legendary cat with nine lives. Every time the doctors gave him no hope, he rebounded. Being diagnosed with illness gave him the impetus he needed to get his life straightened out.

"Bobbie," Teddy said to her that day in the hospital, "don't worry about your hair falling out from the chemotherapy. If you visualize it not to happen, it won't. Picture your hair growing luxuriantly."

After a moment he added, "If people can cure themselves of AIDS by the power of their minds, surely you can keep all your hair."

"Why, I guess you're right," Bobbie said, with forced enthusiasm. "I can *will* my hair not to fall out."

I said nothing, I didn't roll my eyes. I did not want to seem negative. I wished life was really that way and that fate could be changed by positive thinking.

I watched Bobbie. She was smiling sweetly, keeping up the conversation, being positive. Maybe she had learned to die gracefully, like Rick. Her situation seemed hopeless.

I don't think Teddy ever found out that the next day, Bobbie sent her friend Millie out to buy a wig for her. Teddy became very sick and died a few months later. Bobbie's cancer went into remission and she lived another decade.

The Socialites

Todd invited me to Rosedale Plantation, Andy and Beau's country home. I had never spent the weekend at a plantation house before. Todd explained it was not actually an antebellum home--- it had been built in the 1890's-- but it had been restored and furnished as if built 50 years earlier.

Todd and I met at one of Andy and Beau's parties. Todd was terminally cute, about 10 years older than me, but still looked like he was in his early 20's. He was small-framed and thin, like me; unlike me, Todd had golden blond hair and dreamy blue eyes. Sadly for me, he was already in a relationship. Being with him would have been perfect; we were the same size and I could have doubled my wardrobe. Todd embodied the Southern ideal: every move he made, everything he said was socially correct. I doubt he even farted.

Todd lived in an old Victorian cottage, artistically restored, with a much older partner, Leon. Leon seemed vaguely sleazy; he made a fortune in real-estate and bought Todd a house. I think Todd came from money himself. All his friends were wealthy: I was the odd man out.

The parties thrown by Andy and Beau, our hosts at Rosedale Plantation, were wonderful affairs. They were socialites and called the shots in the gay community. They decided who was in, who was out; what to wear, what to eat and where; no one disobeyed their unwritten dictates. We emulated their every move like lemmings. If they'd decided to wear their underwear outside their pants, the rest of us would have done it, too. Andy, I'd been told, was one of the wealthiest men in Baton Rouge.

My great concern was what to wear. Shorts and a T-shirt wouldn't do. Living on a student income, I bought last year's styles on sale at department stores. Even my newest clothes weren't expensive. I assumed I was going to die soon and shopping seemed like a waste of time.

Todd offered to pick me up and drove over in his brand-new sports car. Todd had never seen my apartment or come for one of my dinner parties. My specialty was tofu lasagna with seaweed salad. Only my best friends came to a second dinner party at my place and only the bravest asked for another helping. I hadn't broached the subject of my health with Todd; with all my social handicaps, I had learned to go slowly.

Todd and I rode for about an hour before we came to the old plantation house. He periodically took a drink from the silver flask he carried in his sports coat. "Just to get me in the party mood," he said, with one of his beautiful smiles. "Andy and Beau don't live here at Rosedale, of course, but they usually come up here for weekends and holidays."

It was just getting dark as we arrived. Floodlights artfully illuminated the splendor of the old place; Rosedale Plantation was a two-story white house surrounded on three sides by a verandah. Thick Corinthian pillars supported the moss-covered roof. The house was surrounded by a large garden that was hard to see in the twilight gloom.

Todd opened the massive front door. We entered a foyer with a staircase rising dramatically on the left; the ceiling was two stories high. To our right was the parlor with a sitting room just beyond. Under the stairwell was the door to a ballroom, done in a rich green. Straight ahead was the dining room, its mahogany table spread with silver. The walls were covered with antique paintings and tapestries.

A middle-aged, silver-haired man came over. He was comfortably dressed.

"I don't believe I know you," he said. "I'm Beau." I'd met Andy and Beau briefly at one of their parties; there were a lot of people and Beau could easily be forgiven for not remembering me.

"Oh," I said, "thanks for your hospitality. You have a beautiful place."

"We have fun here," he answered. "Oh," he said, snapping his finger, "you're Todd's friend from Arizona."

"New Mexico," I corrected.

Seconds later, a rather portly man walked in, his cheeks rosy, his eyes twinkling.

"Hey Andy," Todd said.

Andy and Beau poured wine and we all sat down in the den. They were charming and friendly, but I was a little uncomfortable. I sat gingerly on a fine upholstered chair feeling like I was auditioning for a play or interviewing for a job that was above my pay grade. Andy and Beau did their best to put me at ease, though, and embodied Southern hospitality and charm.

An hour or so later they served supper. The dining room was full of silver and porcelain, but we ate take-out pizza in the kitchen with stainless flatware. Maybe they were slumming it to make me feel comfortable.

After dinner, they drank mint juleps and I wandered out on the verandah. Though it was late fall, the evening was warm. I was fighting nervousness and self-doubt. I was an outsider in the gilded society of Rosedale. I thought about Harold who said that he'd always known he was different from everyone else. He assumed it was because he was gay, but after coming out he still felt alienated. Maybe it's the human condition. Maybe some of us are just loners and never fit in.

I wandered back into the house. Andy and Todd were deep in conversation; Beau offered to give me a tour of the house. Beau was in good shape and hadn't added the extra pounds that made Andy a bit plump. It's hard to stay thin in the South, the food is so good.

Beau showed me the bedrooms upstairs. In one room there was an autographed photo of Tennessee Williams, a friend of Beau's uncle. He asked if I was going to sleep with Todd or needed my own room. I didn't know what Todd wanted, he was downstairs; there was no shortage of rooms, so I settled on a canopy bed in a cheery yellow room. It was late and I was too tired to go back downstairs and chat.

I woke up later, looking for a bathroom. I walked into Todd's room in my search. He was sleeping soundly on rose-colored sheets. Todd even slept perfectly. With his blond hair, he looked peaceful, almost angelic.

The next morning I got up early. The others were sleeping in and I took the opportunity to explore the downstairs of Rosedale room by room. It was like being in a museum. Beau got up a little later and found me looking at the artwork in one of the parlors. He made coffee and I followed him into the kitchen. I liked Beau. He was cheery and seemed happy; he was lawyer, recently divorced, with children almost my age. We talked about music and he asked if I had seen the piano. I shook my head and he showed me an old upright piano in an enclosed part of the verandah made into a sun porch.

"Do you play?" he asked, smiling.

"A bit," I hesitated. I can read music but can't play by ear. I noticed an old hymnal.

"Go on!" Beau insisted.

Tentatively I banged out the first hymn. I'm no musician, but Beau didn't seem to mind. Minutes later, the other two were downstairs, unshaved, laughing. We sang those old hymns for over an hour. Whenever I'd falter, they would cheer me on and beg me to play just one more. We laughed and sang until we were hoarse, singing every old hymn we had known from our childhoods.

It was the one time I was invited to the plantation. I did not fit into Andy and Beau's world. I dreamed of it, though, and secretly wished I could be a part of it. Every now and then I went with Todd to one of their parties. I felt awkward, too different. I'd auditioned, but I wasn't what they were looking for. Their world made me tense. I was a hippie born 15 years too late, trapped in the yuppie generation.

My health declined. For the entire gay community, dark days began. A year or so later my friend Rick called me, upset.

"Have you heard about Beau?" he asked. Rick was friends with everyone; he grew up in Baton Rouge and had known Andy and Beau all his life. Rick had recently become ill and moved back home with his mother, Bobbie, when he was not able to work anymore.

"You mean rich Beau, Beau of Andy and Beau?" I had to clarify, because in the South, "Beau" is a common name.

"Yes," he went on. "He's in the hospital with AIDS."

I took a deep breath.

"It's absolutely a secret," Rick said. "Please don't tell anyone. Andy said I could tell you, though, since you're sick."

Those of us who were sick formed a tight circle. There was only one support agency in town, just one doctor who would see AIDS patients, and all of us who were ill crossed paths eventually.

I worried how Beau was coping with the disease. I wondered if it was the first sorrow in his golden life. Beau was handsome and wealthy; he'd had a lot of good luck. Did he know what it was like to be down?

Rick died a year or so after moving back to Baton Rouge. Back in those days, there was no treatment, no medicine. Rick's life was cut short. I saw Beau and Andy at his funeral.

Beau had lost weight and was a little pale, but otherwise looked fine. He seemed as composed as ever. But after the service, as they walked by Rick's open casket, Beau suddenly dropped to his knees, overcome with grief, crying. Andy helped him up and escorted him to a side wing. Beau had been close to Rick, but I couldn't help wondering if it was also for himself he was crying.

I shed some tears at Rick's funeral, I confess. Southern gentlemen don't usually cry in public. Even if your house is burning and the Yankees are shooting at your mother, decorum must be maintained. Emotional restraint is *de rigueur*. I was never sure if it was composure or denial.

I called Beau one day. He seemed glad to hear from me and wanted to come over. I had moved out of my little studio apartment into a converted garage in the Garden   District.

Beau looked well, although he said his blood counts were very low. He chatted and laughed, not talking about his illness. Beau was sicker than me but was caring and concerned about my symptoms. He began visiting regularly, once a week or so, late in the afternoons, sometimes when other friends were calling. Beau always asked how I was feeling but never talked about his own health. I can picture him clearly in my mind, wearing an elegant sweater, sipping a diet cola, talking and laughing.

It's very Southern, very small-town to drop by at your friends' houses. If you know someone well enough, it's not necessary to call first. That would be considered a Yankee affectation. You know when your friends work and when they are free. I lived alone and was glad for the company. Friends would come by, we'd talk and laugh for an hour, maybe have a glass of wine, and then they would be on their way.

Beau died less than a year after Rick. He had no long suffering: he worked until his last day. He never had the typical, emaciated AIDS look Rick had. Andy took Beau to the hospital because of a fever. Beau coughed, his eyelids fluttered, and he was dead. It was the most cosmetic death I had ever heard of: no death rattle, no prolonged pain. Everyone should be so lucky.

Over that last year of his life, I stopped being nervous around Beau and became fond of him. Beau was a nice guy who had led a charmed life--- until that point. He realized he'd been fortunate and wasn't callous towards those who weren't.

Beau's death was like a dull ache; it was the pain of missing someone who has become familiar. From the mid 1980's onward, so many died. My little group of friends and acquaintances diminished by more than half.

I visited Andy about a month after Beau's death. He was taking it very hard. He could not mention Beau's name without crying.

"Beau and I spent a lot of quality time together before his death. Why, we crammed 10 years of fun into that last year," Andy said. "You know, I assumed Beau was working full-time until his death. But according to his secretary, he only worked part-time. And in his desk, I found this."

He showed me a little black book, filled with a dozen names and telephone numbers.

"Do you see the name 'Donald' in there?"

I nodded.

"Well, when Beau died, I decided I'd better call all of Beau's friends in that book, in case they hadn't read it in the paper. That man Donald said he needed to come over and see me."

Andy sighed. "He just came waltzing in here and told me that he had been having a relationship with Beau for the last three years." Andy looked away. "You know, both Beau and I had been married, and we understood that having a gay relationship was not quite the same as the traditional marriages we left. Beau and I were honest with each other. I told that man Donald that I didn't believe him, and I told him to get out of my house."

I said nothing. It was hard to imagine someone being that tacky. Anyone who knew Beau, or claimed to, knew that Andy was grieving. Maybe Beau had been a bit of a rascal, but that didn't diminish Andy's pain.

"Your name was in the book, too," Andy added.

"He stopped by after work," I offered, now unsure if Beau really had been at his office before visiting me.

Driving home, I thought about Beau. Having AIDS was sad but it had not really changed his life. The party lasted until his death. He lived past 50, which, in those days, was quite an accomplishment. Beau lived under a lucky star and led a full life.

Andy, on the other hand, was a changed man. He suffered some business setbacks, I was told. He became serious and almost melancholy. He was very reflective. Andy knew his money could not bring back Beau or prolong either of their lives.

"I know I will never love again," Andy confided wistfully, another time I visited him.

I did not think he was being melodramatic. Some people only love once in their lives, pouring out love so deeply that when it is expended the well is dry.

Several years later, a mutual friend called to tell me that Andy had passed away. I don't believe he ever found love again.

The Museum

"You shall not die, you shall live again forever." I read the words, written above the entrance to the mummy's tomb, and fought back unexpected tears. The inscription moved me. "I shall not die," I said to myself. I had been battling disease for what seemed like a long time. In my heart, I could not believe that I was going to die. Maybe everyone feels that way; it might have been denial on my part. But my instincts told me that I was going to live, that the nightmare would end. I was afraid of dying, but sometimes I believed I would survive the night.

I stared at the message on the archway, translated in big black Roman letters. I thought about the person that had written them, 3,000 years ago. What comforting words, what a lovely idea, to live forever. Once I'd believed in an afterlife; but at that time, I was unsure. I longed to see my friends again and be with the people I loved. So many of them were dead: Wayne, Rick, Alberto, the socialites. I did not care about living forever, but I wanted to see my buddies again.

Tracy waited with me at the opening of the ancient sepulcher. He was fascinated with all things Egyptian. It had been his idea to visit this exhibit at the museum down in New Orleans. I looked at his handsome face and smiled. He was a few years older than me and looked like the Marlboro man; his features were chiseled. He came from old Texas oil money and was an urban cowboy from his black moustache to his roper boots.

Tracy was very religious: he was not happy about being gay and had even been married. But he was learning, growing, and I knew his salvation would come when he could leave the rigid beliefs of his childhood. I did not love him, not romantically, but I liked spending time with him. Tracy was thoughtful and always polite; he was a good listener. He spoke with a slight Austin drawl.

We entered the mummy's tomb. I wondered about the pharaoh's ancient religion, his cult of immortality. Were his beliefs kind, universal, or did they only help a few? Was it like Judaism or Christianity, the faiths I was familiar with? The problem with some organized religions is that they force you to come to definite conclusions with insufficient evidence. Who could know which religion was right, or if there was an afterlife? At that time, I wasn't sure if I believed in God. It took me years to come to a mature understanding of the deity. Clearly, there is no old man with a white beard living on a cloud.

Most religions are similar and have some version of the Golden Rule. If a religion doesn't mandate kindness, then it's not useful and should be discarded.

St. John of the Cross wrote that we will be judged on how much we have loved. I once asked a friend who was a Lutheran pastor what that meant. She answered, "It's not as if there is an interrogation or accounting when you die. No, it's like you are taking a trip, and the only thing you can bring back home is your treasure. When you die, be sure you have brought the best with you. The only thing worth carrying our entire journey is love, it's the only thing that matters or lasts."

Coming from an interfaith background, I learned to pick and choose. While there are disadvantages to being Jewish, in some ways I was better suited for it. I appreciate the emphasis on education and ethics. The food is delicious and no one minds if you talk with your hands. You can even sprinkle your speech with Yiddish and say things that you wouldn't say in English. Of course, there is the whole discrimination thing, as I found out when I traveled in Europe. France is lousy with anti-Semites.

Tracy struggled with fundamentalist religion. I wanted to shake him, to help him stop tormenting himself. "Why support a concept of God that does not support you?" I asked.

Tracy knew I was sick and it did not matter. He wasn't romantically interested in me. Sometimes, though, he would hold me for hours in the evening. Those were my happiest hours, being in someone's arms. It was only in a warm embrace that I could find rest and peace of mind. Always an insomniac, I fall asleep the moment someone holds me. In Tracy's strong arms I relaxed. It didn't matter that he didn't love me; it was enough spending time together. I respected Tracy, although others criticized him, considering him "uptight," a "closet case." I knew how hard he was working and how far he had come.

Tracy examined the writing on the wall of the mummy's tomb. He could decipher some of the hieroglyphics and told me what they meant. The tunnel to the tomb narrowed, and for an instant, Tracy held me close. Nervous that someone would come, he broke away.

Finally we came upon the mummy. I stared, repulsed and fascinated at the same time. I looked at everything the ancients had placed with him. He had not eaten the dried food or drunk the wine. I wondered if his soul had found rest. Had he loved greatly during his life and had he carried love with him to the other side?

Months earlier I had been to Rick's funeral and had stared at the body of my friend. As I walked past the open coffin, paying my last respects, I reached down to touch his hand. It was so cold, not the feverish hand I'd held just days earlier.

Suddenly I wanted to reach out and touch the mummy, to see if he was cold, all these centuries after his death. Exhibiting his corpse seemed like a desecration. Once he'd been a living being, now his remains were in a museum. I turned to Tracy and told him I wanted to leave. He understood, perhaps also affected by the melancholy of the tomb. Preserving the body did not nullify the reality of death.

The mummy was surrounded by beautiful things. He'd no doubt been surrounded by luxury when he was alive. I hoped he'd enjoyed it. You have to enjoy life here and now: it's all anyone has. A glorious tomb, a shrine to death, is pointless.

As we left the museum, I looked again at the inscription at the entrance. "You shall not die, you shall live again forever." If only those words were true! If only death was not final.

I thought about my desire to live. What made me cling to life so tenaciously? I was not a pharaoh, just an ordinary man; it seemed like the best and most beautiful people had already died. Why should I be spared the fate of so many others? If death didn't come when I was young, it would come when I was old. Did a few years one way or another really matter?

I looked at Tracy and thought about the friends in my life, the people I loved. Their friendship and affection was the only thing that was important to me. R

Relationships were why I kept going. Love is life's most important task. I had golden moments that eased all the pain. At times I was so happy, happier, I thought, than anyone had a right to be. To use religious terminology, I felt blessed.

I held Tracy's hand as he drove home. A voice on the radio sang, "I only hope that you will hold me now, till I can gain control again." Back at Tracy's house, he held me, and the song echoed in my mind.

Tracy fell in love with someone a few weeks after our museum trip and I saw less of him. He no longer held me. I was not angry at him, but I did miss his gentle affection.

About a year later I went to visit Tracy in the hospital; he called to tell me he was sick. His new friend took care of him until his death a year later.

"He suffered so much," his partner said. "He was ready to go: blind, barely weighing 100 pounds, he passed away with a smile on his lips."

I dream about Tracy every now and then, always telling him, "You shall not die, you shall live again forever." I say the words over and over, like a chant or a strange incantation.

Halloween

In south Louisiana, there's always a reason to celebrate. The year starts with revelry at New Year's. After that comes Mardi Gras, a season of masked balls, pageants, and parades. Next is Easter, when you can start wearing white. Memorial Day is the beginning of summer, punctuated by the Fourth of July. Due to the heat things calm down in August. Labor Day, with the craziness of Southern Decadence Day, a celebration unique to New Orleans, inaugurates the fall and winter party seasons. There is Halloween, Thanksgiving, and Christmas. Of all the celebrations, though, Halloween was my favorite. In New Orleans, it rivals Mardi Gras.

Southerners love to spend Halloween at haunted plantation homes. There's no shortage of them; every Halloween I was in the South I went to a different ghost-filled antebellum mansion. One of the most haunted sites in the country is in south Louisiana, a plantation called the Myrtles. It was built on a sacred Indian burial spot so it has had literally hundreds of years of spirit activity. A friend of mine, a bright young journalist, agreed to spend the night there and do an article for the newspaper. He could never bring himself to talk about what he experienced, he was too shaken.

Although I never spent the night at the Myrtles, I can attest to its creepiness. I first visited the Myrtles with Martin, a friend of mine from the university who taught horticulture. It was late and I was tired, so I went ahead of the tour guide to one of the parlors and sat down. I briefly closed my eyes when I heard the rocking chair next to me start to move. I smiled to myself, sure it was a gag. I looked all around for the string that I assumed was pulling it, but found nothing. By the time the Martin caught up to me, the chair had stopped its spontaneous movement.

Martin was from the Southwest, too, from West Texas. He was sweet, understanding and a good listener. Martin was one of the first people in Baton Rouge I told about my health situation.

"I thought I had problems," he said, gently patting me on the shoulder. Martin and I became close because of a mutual friend.   At a party, Martin came over and introduced himself to me.   He said, "I hear you're a member of the club, too."

"What do you mean?" I asked.

"You are an official member of the 'Tim's ex-boyfriends Society,'" Martin explained.

"Oh," I said. "Are there a lot of us?"

Martin laughed. "Well, let's just say if you're young, intelligent, and reasonably nice-looking, you've had at least one date with Tim. I went out with him a few times."

I'd met Tim the first spring I was in Baton Rouge. Tim had moved to the South a year before me. In a short time, he made himself known as a champion of progressive causes. A Ph.D. as well as an attorney, Tim was smart and expressed himself clearly. Say what you will about Yankees, and most Southerners have something to say on the subject--- they know how to get things done. Tim was no exception. He had Baton Rouge organized within months of his arrival. He formed a group for gay rights and another to care for people with HIV. Tim knew a lot about AIDS.

"Before I came here, I was living on the East Coast," he told me one evening over coffee. "The epidemic was just starting to hit New York City. The way I look at it, I was spared. It would have just been a matter of time before I caught it."

Tim and I went out a few times; I liked him. At first he was friendly but then found me too superficial. Tim moved on to greener pastures. Maybe he sensed I was needy and inexperienced. My feelings were hurt, of course.

"By, the way, how long did you and Tim date?" Martin asked.

"I wouldn't say we were dating," I answered defensively. "We just went out a couple or three times."

"Three times? That's long- term for Tim. You should file for palimony."

We   both   laughed.   Martin   was   funny.

"Have you met Tim's new boyfriend, Carl? He's in the science department," Martin continued.

"Tim moves fast," I said.

"Well, Tim has a lot going for him; you must think so or you wouldn't have gone out with him. You'll meet Carl, I'm sure."

My chance to meet Carl came the following Halloween when Martin and I were invited to a party. Naturally, it was held at a plantation house that was rumored to be lousy with restless spirits.

But at this Halloween event, there were only two people I wished had been ghosts, Tim and his new boyfriend, Carl. Carl was tall and fair, with salt-and-pepper hair he insisted was still brown.

"They've been together three or four months," Martin whispered to me in astonishment. "This must be serious."

"Wow. I just had three dates with him," I said.

Tim had wounded my pride when he stopped returning my calls. Standing in line at the buffet, Tim and Carl came over. Tim said a cheery "hello," and I turned away from him without speaking. It was adolescent on my part, but that's how I am.

"Jerk," Carl muttered. Martin and I smiled at each other. I was the petty one for not speaking; still, Martin and I began to giggle uncontrollably. Neither of us needed liquor to act silly.

School kept me busy and I spent many weekends in New Orleans. I put Tim and Carl out my mind. Several months later, I saw Martin on campus. He was not alone; he was with Carl, Tim's boyfriend. They were standing very close.

"Tim broke up with Carl," Martin explained.

I laughed. "Of course. Welcome to the club," I told Carl. I had not forgotten how Carl called me a name at the Halloween party. I soon learned I'd misjudged Carl---or maybe he'd misjudged me. The three of us went out to supper and had fun. Martin and Carl fell in love and moved in together.

I begin to see Carl frequently on campus. I lived near the university and he sometimes stopped by to see me on his way home. As the months passed, Carl and I saw each other a lot. I don't remember what we chatted about. Carl didn't want me to talk about my illness. I think he was afraid for himself. He told me, "You haven't been promiscuous and yet you are sick. I worry about me and Martin." It was an understandable reaction.

Sex was problematic in the age of AIDS, but I was content just being held. Harold and I spent hours just holding each other. Gradually, Carl and I began to do the same thing. Often, late in the afternoon, we would hold each other close, rarely speaking.

"I don't have this with Martin," Carl confided. "We have great sex, but not this cuddling."

"Do you love me?" I asked.

Carl was silent.

"I think I might love you," I mused. "Are we having some kind of affair? Is this unfair to Martin?"

"I wonder about that myself," he finally responded. "There is something between us."

We continued to be close, to have feelings for each other, not putting those feelings into words. Not every friendship has to have a name; there are different ways of loving. That was a tenet of gay liberation in the era of AIDS. We were creating our own kinds of family.

One hot summer afternoon, a group of us went out rafting on a nearby river. It was relaxing and fun; we took a picnic with us and ate on the banks. Martin couldn't go; Carl and I came back exhausted and took a nap. Carl held me close. As the setting sun cast shadows on the wall, he started talking.

"It's almost like a dance, isn't it," Carl said.

"What?"

"Oh, you know, relationships. I could leave Martin and move in with you, and then that would last until you or I found someone else, and it would just keep going. There's Tim, who falls in love, moves them in, then moves them out. At some time you have to make a commitment to someone, you have to say, even if I am attracted to someone else, I will stay with my partner. You make a promise and try to keep it."

Carl and Martin had been together for a couple of years by that time. Carl was right, I thought, it could be a dance, a never-ending chain of lovers. Constant change didn't sound like a recipe for happiness. In his way, Carl was putting a boundary between us, a limit to our friendship. I understood that and respected him.

Carl turned to me. "And you," he said, "what do you want? There are guys interested in you, but you stay single. What are you looking for?"

His question troubled me. What was I looking for, and why could I never be happy with anyone I was dating? Was it them or me? Did I believe I was unlovable because of my illness and keep myself emotionally unavailable? What if others weren't as afraid of me as I was of them? Maybe I had used my disease as an excuse to be alone.

The following fall, Martin, Carl and I decided to go to a Halloween party in drag. Naturally, the party was held at a haunted plantation. Carl said that when you go in drag, you unconsciously bring out a side of yourself. Tall, masculine Carl went as a ballerina. Martin, from West Texas, went as a honky-tonk angel with big red hair and a square dancing skirt. I went as the widow, wearing a long black dress and flowing black veil.

One evening when Martin was working late, Carl and I ate a simple cold supper of salad, fruit, and yogurt. For a rare moment, I was silent, thinking about Tim, who went in and out of relationships with ease. Tim brought Martin, Carl and me together without knowing it. I wondered about myself and my own fear of committing. Dealing with AIDS was like having to come out all over again. I had a secret that made me different. Maybe everyone has AIDS, in some way or another: maybe that is why people are so afraid of it. Just like people are frightened of the side of them that is gay, they are scared by whatever AIDS means to them. AIDS can be a symbol of disease, sex, mortality, and everything that is unknowable and dark.

As we ate, the kitchen grew dark, but each of us was too absorbed in thought to turn the light on. The phone rang and we were both startled. It was Martin. As he talked, Carl looked crestfallen. He hung up the phone.

"Tim has just been hospitalized with AIDS," Carl said. "He's practiced safe sex for years--- he was the one who told me about it."

Carl left my place in a hurry. Tim's illness was a blow to our political fight for rights. It was a sad lesson: any indiscretion you had 10 or 15 years earlier could have fatal consequences.

Tim's parents came down to take care of him but he couldn't bring himself to tell them that he was gay or what his illness was. The activist wasn't able to be honest with his own mom and dad. I don't judge him for that. There was so much stigma back then; there still is.

I did the dishes in semi-darkness. I was sad about the devastation of our community. It hit all strata, from the lounge lizards to the clergy to the politicians. Yet somehow we all found it in us to keep going. I had moments of peace, times of respite. My love was strong not only for those who were alive but for those who had died. At times I even let myself think that there might be something beyond the grave, a life to come, when we would be reunited.

One cold winter night, I woke up from a strange dream. Carl, the scientist, one of the most rational people I have ever known, said: "You know they have proved that there is life on other planets."

In my dream I was incredulous. "Carl, you can't be serious. You're a scientist."

"It's true," he assured me. "There is a far-off planet, a beautiful place of sensitivity and love. No one judges us there. It's the planet where we are from."

I listened as Carl continued.

"We were sent here to bring them our gift. And now some of us are being called back to our world."

In my dream it suddenly became clear to me: this illness was our summons to go home, to return to a place of love and acceptance.

My eyes were damp when I woke up. If only, I thought, it was really like that. If there were such a planet, such a paradise, where we were all together, where we were free to love and to be ourselves. I longed for a land where we were understood and did not have to pretend, where we did not have to explain anything.

Tim died a few months later. Martin passed away several years after that. Carl remains in good health.

Cary

Ruth's partner worked on Saturday afternoons so she and I often got together then. Ruth was my age, with short brown hair, and looked slightly boyish. She worked in a warehouse and wrote poetry during her coffee breaks. On Saturdays she sometimes read me what she'd written that week; her writing was pretty good.

One hot summer afternoon, someone knocked on Ruth's door. Her air conditioning was not working and we were wearing as little as we could. She set down her notebook and sighed. "If this heat keeps up, I swear I'm going to answer the door naked. That will surprise the missionaries." We laughed.

Ruth said "hello," and her neighbor Cary came in. I hurriedly slipped on a T-shirt and shook his hand. Cary was slender and tan with sandy hair; he wasn't short and he wasn't tall. He didn't look like a movie star but he was cute, probably about 21 or 22, at the juncture in his life when he was going from youth to manhood. I was 25 and had already made that transition.

Cary had come to return a book. Like Ruth, he loved to read. The three of us chatted for a while, then he went back to home. He told me where he lived and invited me to stop by. After Cary left, Ruthie confided, "You know, darlin', he's HIV positive too."

Back when AIDS was new, the gay and lesbian community was tightly knit, especially in that small Southern town. HIV was a secret most of us didn't keep from our closest friends. This information was safe; no told the larger world. This was partly out of discretion and sensitivity, but also due to the fact that it would have been social suicide to admit that you knew someone with AIDS. People lost their jobs for things like that.

One afternoon when Ruth was busy, I visited Cary. He was going to trade school and lived in a clean, tidy apartment that was even smaller than mine. He was sitting on his bed reading some New Age book. We didn't engage in endless conversation but began a gentle friendship. I can still remember every detail: how he looked, his touch, his scent.

Sometimes, we'd talk afterwards. Fate had not been kind to Cary. He'd had a hard childhood; he was abused and neglected. I think he finished his last year of high school living in a car. He was amazingly even-tempered and grown-up; he showed no bitterness. Cary did not dwell on the past and never talked about being HIV positive. Maybe he was ashamed or maybe it was just one more adversity in a life that had not been easy. I don't know how he managed; I never asked how he paid for his tuition.

As a teenager Cary wanted to join the navy, but there was "Don't Ask Don't Tell" so that wasn't possible. He learned how to cut hair. When he finished school he wanted to be a hair dresser in a high-class salon. He planned on living in a big city: he said he was going to dance and party all night long.

One day, Ruth told me Cary left for Atlanta. We never said goodbye. That wasn't the nature of our friendship. I could say that Cary was a simple man but that sounds condescending; it's more accurate to say he wasn't complicated. Cary was no drama queen. We called one another every now and then and he was always saving up money to come out and visit.

Ruth and I have always kept in touch. She's still sweet; she's still cute and boyish. Ruth always asks how I'm feeling and if things are OK. We laugh about the old days, our former lives, and of course our former romances. She has a new love now but is still friends with her former girlfriend.

Once, shortly after I moved to San Diego, I asked Ruthie what I always asked. "Have you heard from Cary in Atlanta? How's he doing?"

Ruth fell silent and a feeling of dread came over me. "Darlin'," she said softly, "I didn't tell you?"

I braced myself. "Is he dead?"

It was the inevitable question and I got the sad answer. My friend Jack in L.A. says that after you lose 50 friends you stop counting. I don't agree. You keep counting and every loss hurts. It doesn't get any easier. The wrong people die: jerks and dictators thrive and seem to live forever. God has some explaining to do.

The heart has its own seasons and sometimes I ache for Cary. Cary wanted so little from life. He was gentle and kind. I love you Cary, and I miss you. I promise to remember... always.

The Perfect Couple

The South maintains its own north/south distinctions. Tennessee is southern, but Mississippi is the real South, the Deep South. Within Louisiana there is also a north and south. This divide is so strong that Louisiana is the only state without a freeway running top to bottom. The southern part of Louisiana, where I lived, is French and Catholic, populated by Cajuns and Creoles. In south Louisiana people make sure there's plenty of good food and drink; New Orleans is the City That Care Forgot. The northern half of the state is Protestant, non-drinking, and decidedly red-neck.

Shreveport is hardly New Orleans. I wondered why Dale and Pierre, the couple I was going to visit, moved there. They relocated from Southern California where Dale had been a television soap-opera actor: now he was selling real-estate. Pierre was the chef at a French restaurant. I hadn't met them; they were friends of Jack, my L.A. buddy. Jack was in his early 50's, relaxed and easy-going. He was visiting Louisiana and before coming to New Orleans, he wanted to see his old friends. Jack invited me to Shreveport to meet Dale and Pierre.

I followed Jack's directions and came to a charming Victorian house in an affluent part of town. Dale and Pierre were clearly doing well. I looked forward to spending the weekend in a real house. My student apartment was shabby and cramped.

When I rang the bell, Jack answered the door. He took me down a long hall to the kitchen where he introduced me to Dale and Pierre. Dale was a tall, Nordic blond with a well-proportioned, muscular body. His smile showed perfect teeth and his voice was deep and sonorous. I wondered why he'd ever left Hollywood: he had movie star looks and what they call "presence." Pierre was from southern France: his haunting eyes were as black as his thick, curly hair.

They were perfect, I thought to myself, absolutely perfect. They weren't going to be featured on "Lifestyles of the Rich and Famous," but they had a bourgeois life that I aspired to. No doubt they had worked hard, but some happy star smiled over them.

They'd been together for years, building a home and investment portfolio. I wondered if someday I'd have a life like theirs--- I doubted it. So young and yet so cynical, Jack always used to say about me.

Tired from the long drive on a barely paved two-lane state highway, I went to bed early. The guest bedroom was lovely with tasteful floral wall-paper and an antique headboard and dresser. I'd been asleep for an hour or so when Jack settled in next to me. The house was large but there was just one guest room. We talked a little; he told me about the activities planned the next day. I drifted back to sleep happily, thinking about the perfect couple, Dale and Pierre.

We got up early the next morning. Pierre was already in the kitchen cooking Eggs Benedict for breakfast. It was early autumn and the weather was still warm, so we ate outside on the patio. In the afternoon, we soaked in the hot tub and drank mimosas. It was almost perfect, like some happy dream. My health problems didn't belong in Dale and Pierre's sunny world; it felt like a dark cloud hung over me. I was an outsider.

It didn't help that they asked questions contrasting my life with theirs. What did I do--- a student? Still, at my age? What did I study? Didn't I know that teachers don't make any money? Why not get an M.B.A.? Why wasn't I in law school? That's a question I've asked myself a lot over the years. Of course, the 1980's, the Reagan era, was the decade of the yuppie.

My interest in literature and language has always seemed impractical to most people. I've always loved to read; I'm bookish. I like traveling. I wouldn't have been happy doing anything but teaching. Because of my poor health I wasn't planning for the long term, anyway.

But I could not really explain myself to Dale and Pierre. At that time in my life, I was so impressed by the external. Their life was golden, and mine was silver, or at least silver-plate; maybe just stainless. The weekend was lovely, and I felt sad driving home. The success of their lives touched me.

About six months later I got a phone call from Jack. He had just talked to Dale and Pierre: something was wrong. My heart broke when I heard the news. Dale had AIDS. We had just been up there and he didn't look sick. I was sad, disbelieving. The perfect couple-- how could this happen to them? How would they deal with it, how would they cope? They did not know how to suffer: their lives had been so good up to that point. Jack asked me to go up to Shreveport and visit them.

It was a couple of months before I could get away. I was unprepared for the change in their lives. Dale had gone to a hospital in Houston to begin treatment. The doctors said his case was hopeless and he had only months to live. Dale gave a television interview for the local news in Texas and was assured that his real name would not be used. But the interview appeared on the national news later that week with his full name. His infuriated parents called, cursing him, telling him that God's wrath was being visited upon him for his wicked life-style. Dale lost all his real estate business: clients in Shreveport abandoned him.

Dale and Pierre's lives had become a nightmare. Dale's health insurance was canceled and he owed tens of thousands of dollars in medical bills. The owner of the restaurant where Pierre worked fired him, knowing that Dale was his roommate. Pierre began to show signs of illness as well. The people of that Southern town acted like a lynch mob, sending them hate mail and making threatening phone calls.

There were no cars in the driveway of their house when I got there: bill collectors repossessed them. Pierre had to ride a bicycle to get groceries and medicine. There was a for-sale sign in the front yard. Because they lost their jobs, Dale and Pierre were unable to make house payments and their home was being foreclosed. Inside, their house was almost empty. Dale and Pierre had to sell their furniture to buy food and medicine. All the pictures were gone from the walls, except for one. It was a pencil drawing of a young woman, stretched out on a sofa. I had once asked about it: it caught my eye the first time I visited. *La fille s'allonge*, it was called. Dale knew the artist.

Their friends had mostly abandoned them, except for one devoted woman, Angela. I met her the first time I visited Dale and Pierre. She was a pretty, successful businesswoman. Angela had paid a price for friendship: she had let it slip out at work that she knew Dale and Pierre and was fired. In those days simply knowing someone with AIDS could cost your job. It probably still can.

Angela answered the door when I rang. She looked tired and motioned for me to be quiet, both Dale and Pierre were sleeping. She led me into the kitchen where I'd been served gourmet meals just a few months earlier.

"As soon as Dale is well enough to travel, they are going to go live with a friend in California," Angela told me. "They still know someone from Dale's Hollywood days."

"This can't be happening," I said, in disbelief.

Pierre came down the stairs, looking tired and thin. He hugged me feebly.

"Thanks for coming," he said. He lit up a joint, and he and Angela smoked. I wanted to stop the tragedy unfolding before me. There was nothing I or anyone could do and I felt helpless.

"This house is cursed," Pierre said, his accent heavier than usual. "The neighbors told us a witch used to live here. When we moved in, one room was painted all black and there was a pentagram on the wall."

Thinking about Dale and Pierre's bad luck, it was possible, at least for a moment, to believe in witches and curses.

"Dale and Pierre were the first people to have AIDS in Shreveport," Angela muttered. "But they've had company. Other people have it. Even here, in this little God-forsaken town."

I said nothing as Angela continued. "I'm in a special high risk group," she continued. "What do you call a woman who used to be a drug user and has dated bisexual men? What kind of special risk group is that?" Angela laughed darkly.

I asked to see Dale. He was lying upstairs in the guest room, in the antique bed I had once slept in. He was pale and thin. Dale spoke softly, with difficulty.

"I need another one of those," he said, pointing to the bottle of tranquilizers by his bed. I opened the bottle, and gave him one.

"Two, I need two," he said.

Dale complained of nausea and headaches and said the tranquillizers helped relieve the pain. It was more than the pain of his body, I felt sure: it was the pain of someone who had been handsome and successful and whose world had come quickly crashing down. This should not have happened, I said over and over to myself. Dale and Pierre should have been spared.

Dale fell asleep even as I was talking to him. I found myself saying meaningless words in a low whisper, hoping to comfort him. I went back downstairs where Pierre, Angela and I ate supper in silence.

I did some shopping and errands for Dale and Pierre; as a gesture of thanks, Dale gave me the last picture hanging on their walls. *La fille s'allonge* is in my bedroom. Dale and Pierre finally got enough money to go to California when Dale was well enough to travel. Dale died shortly after they got there. I lost contact with Angela and don't know what happened to Pierre.

The perfect couple. It should not have happened to them. Yet it did happen: it happened over and over. The same sad story kept repeating itself. The rich, the poor, the middle class; lonely singles and perfect couples all died. The lives of Dale and Pierre were ordinary, mundane. But when I was young, they seemed like the summit of happiness. Their love, their lot, was bourgeois but no less beautiful for it.

So many were dying. Yet the nation at large was either oblivious or downright hostile. Our pain was marginalized, condemned, AIDS wasn't something that happened to nice people. No cure, no treatment was on the horizon. We had to advocate for and defend ourselves. By the end of the 1980's, we were. In New York and San Francisco, we were taking to the streets.

Jimmy

Food is taken as seriously as religion in the South, especially in Cajun country. The cuisine is rich and spicy; *roux*, a brown sauce, is the base. Along the Gulf Coast, the seafood is fresh and there's no shortage of shrimp and oysters. Gumbo, a seafood soup made with okra is one specialty; jambalaya is a delicious dish of chicken and rice. Some dishes are exotic, like *boudin*, blood sausage, and hog's head cheese. They also serve *cervelles*, brains. I learned to appreciate crawfish, which look like bugs, and I was hooked on cheese grits the first time I ate them. Eating is a sensory experience and many restaurants feature live Cajun music.

One of the tricks religious organizations use to draw students is to have a shrimp and crawfish boil. I met Jimmy and Chris at an event like that. Jimmy was almost two years younger than me, getting his Master's degree in engineering. He was a snappy dresser and I never saw him wear a wrinkled shirt. Considering the humidity of the South, that's quite an accomplishment. He spoke with a Southern twang and had a gentle demeanor.

Chris was studying French, like me, and he and Jimmy were best friends since childhood. The three of us shared a similar sense of humor and neither of them minded my sarcastic tongue. Chris was in the process of coming out, Jimmy was straight. When Chris headed off for France I started hanging around Jimmy more; he and I became buddies.

Jimmy knew my health status but wasn't freaked out. He liked my friends and started stopping by my place in the late afternoon. It's very Southern to stop by, and Jimmy was always welcome. He and I enjoyed the same things: movies, folk music, politics. Jimmy was always ready to do something, whether it grabbing a cup of chicory coffee and a beignet or taking a quick trip to New Orleans. We shared worries, too; we wondered if we would find jobs after grad school. As an engineer, his chances were better than mine.

"Your friend Jimmy's not as straight as you think," Anne, Rick's sister, once said to me.

"Sure he's straight," I protested. "He's dating Linda." I'd met Linda a couple of times but didn't know her well.

"You're clueless," Anne said, with a sigh.

Bobbie, Anne and Rick's mother, liked Jimmy; if she wondered about his sexuality, she never said.

Bobbie, Jimmy and I went down to New Orleans to see Pete and Millie; Pete and Millie liked Jimmy, too. The five of us went out to eat a lot; Pete and Millie knew the best restaurants. Baton Rouge has plenty of good places to eat but the cafes of New Orleans are world-famous. Lord, I ate well in those days. New Orleans restaurants can make simple sandwiches, po'boys, or red beans and rice into a feast.

One Halloween, Jimmy wanted to go to see one of the area's many haunted plantations.

"You can hold my hand if you get scared," he teased.

I told him I'd take him up on that and Jimmy just smiled. When we arrived at the creepy old place, I hesitated for a minute. I believe that it's possible for spirits to come back after death and return to the places they loved. In those early days of AIDS I thought a lot about death and the afterlife. We all did. While time has changed my perspective on many things, I still believe it's possible for the dead to visit the living.

The old plantation was crowded. We had to make our way carefully through the house since it was very dark. There were the usual cheesy gimmicks, from peeled grapes for eyeballs to teenagers dressed like axe murderers jumping out from hidden doorways. I grabbed Jimmy's hand once and squeezed it hard because I'd told him I would. When we left, we were both laughing.

"You're crazy," Jimmy said, in his sweet Southern twang, giving me a powerful hug.

On the drive home we talked and laughed. "Hey, how's Linda doing?" I asked. "You haven't mentioned her lately."

"We broke up," he said.

"I'm sorry. Why didn't you tell me?"

"It's not that big a deal," he answered.

The next week, Jimmy was visiting me when Joe, Rick's friend, dropped by. Joe sat with Rick while he was in the hospital. Joe was loyal to the end and was a great support to Bobbie, Rick's mother. After Rick died, Joe and I became friends.

I wasn't sure what Joe did for a living; he was good to guys with AIDS. He personally made sure no one was in the hospital all alone. He looked a little like a young Santa Claus: he was overweight and his cheeks were ruddy. His beard was light brown and his pale blue eyes twinkled when he laughed, which was often. Joe was saintly, in my eyes. I didn't know about his spiritual practices but Joe lived out the best message of all religions, kindness to those in need.

Jimmy, Joe and I chatted for a few minutes, but Jimmy had a test the next day so he left. Joe smiled at me.

"I like your new boyfriend," he said.

"He's isn't my boyfriend, he's straight," I protested. "But you're not the only one who thinks he and I are a couple." Several years earlier I had a straight friend who was teased mercilessly for hanging around me. I hoped my friendship wasn't going to cause trouble for Jimmy. In the days before "Will and Grace" it wasn't cool to have a gay buddy.

Joe shrugged. "Whatever makes you happy. He's cute."

"Like you'd notice," I said. Joe had been married for years.

"Why wouldn't I notice if someone is cute?" Joe asked. "I'm not blind."

"But you're straight. It's different for you."

"I don't know who you've been talking to, but I'm not straight," Joe said. "You think you're the only gay guy with AIDS?"

I hope my face didn't register the surprise I felt. Maybe Anne was right and I was clueless. It had never occurred to me that Joe might be gay or have AIDS.

"Your wife?" I asked.

"She's my best friend. She knows all about me. We got married young, before I realized it wouldn't work. Now we're in too much of a rut to get divorced." He sighed. "When the doctor told me I had AIDS I just laughed. My life has been a roller coaster. I've faced death more than once. If you don't mind me saying so, Jimmy likes you a lot."

"I'm sorry you have AIDS, Joe," I said, ignoring his comment about Jimmy. "That's rough." I suspected that there were many guys like Joe in the South, gay men who got married because it was the thing to do. Joe didn't seem bitter. Humor was his way of coping; I can't remember when he wasn't smiling, telling jokes. There are worse ways to deal with stress.

I told Bobbie about my conversation with Joe. She knew him better than I did and had never mentioned him being gay or having AIDS. Bobbie was very discrete.

"Yes, I heard Joe is gay and has AIDS. But you hear a lot of things, and what does it matter? He helps so many people," she said. Bobbie was a wise woman and much of what she advised has stayed with me. When I was worried how one particular person would react when they learned of my illness, Bobbie told me, "you'll find most people won't kick you when you're down." She was right.

"Bobbie," I said, "what exactly does Joe do? I know he spends a lot of time visiting guys in the hospital, but how does he make his living?" When I complained once about having nausea, a frequent problem for me in those years, Joe brought me some cookies. They calmed my stomach and gave me an appetite.

"I wouldn't know," Bobbie said. "Some things a person is better off not knowing."

In the South, it's not polite to ask a lot of personal questions. Joe traveled a lot but didn't say where he went or what he did. He was gone for weeks at a time.

Once I commended Joe for all the hard work he did with AIDS patients. "I had to get some kind of a job when I got out of prison," he answered. I didn't ask why he was in jail because it didn't matter. He had paid his dues for whatever he'd done.

Another time Joe asked me point blank, "You know what I do, don't you?"

"You take care of AIDS patients and you're a great cook. That's all I want to know, Joe." The one rule I made for our friendship was that he not tell me how he made   a   living.

A couple of weeks later, Joe came by again when Jimmy was at my place. Joe wanted to say goodbye before a business trip. He mentioned he was looking for a new business travel agent; Jimmy's sister was one. Joe began doing business with her.

"What does he do?" Jimmy asked me, when Joe left.

"I don't know," I said, "and I don't want to know." Joe was a free spirit and reminded me of a good-natured friend I'd had in Albuquerque. Larry had no visible means of support and I never asked how he lived. Larry helped me get a job at an Indian art gallery that helped me pay for college and my Master's degree.

Jimmy and I watched TV together while we studied. Several weeks after Halloween, the news was on and we had our books in front of us. "Do you like me?" Jimmy asked.

"Sure I like you," I said. "I see you almost every day. Too bad you're not..." I stopped myself.

"I can't tell if you like me," Jimmy said. "You hug me, you hold my hand--- you're so damn frustrating."

Finally I understood and held Jimmy close. It was hard for him to say the words. Jimmy was sweet and soft-spoken: I didn't know how much he was struggling with his identity. I talk a lot, probably too much, but Jimmy said little and I was never sure what was going on inside. Sometimes I felt like I didn't know Jimmy at all. Maybe one person never really knows another; at times you don't even know yourself. Sometimes still water is just still water, sometimes it runs deep.

Jimmy and I began a long, uncertain courtship. Because we were both students we didn't know where our jobs would take us. We tried not to think about the future, but that's impossible. Most of the time I didn't think I had a future---the present was the only thing that mattered. Jimmy seemed to be content with that.

He was reluctant to tell his family about being gay. The South is conservative and Jimmy was afraid of rejection. It's hazardous just being a liberal. Jimmy often went with me to doctor's visits and listened to my complaints and fears. Because he was healthy I always assumed everything was OK for him.

One evening Jimmy was more quiet than usual. I never knew how hard to pry; I wanted to know his feelings but I wanted him to have space, privacy. Finally he told me what was on his mind.

"I don't want you to die," he said, finally.

Jimmy liked traveling and we went to England one summer. Through the challenges of overseas flights, taxis, and indecipherable maps, he kept his humor and good-natured disposition. Towards the end of one exhausting day, though, Jimmy got mad and put his foot down. "You are not going to drag me to one more old cathedral. I just can't stand to see another dang church."

Jimmy and I stayed close for many years; his career took him to a small town in Texas and I moved to the coast. I worried I couldn't get good medical care in a small town.

Gradually we drifted apart. It was until we were far away that I had more insight into Jimmy's struggles. I'd been so absorbed with my own problems I wasn't always aware of his difficulties. Jimmy didn't, couldn't, tell me some things; it wasn't till many years later I learned how much he suffered from depression. Like so many who struggle with that terrible illness, he occasionally tried to self-medicate. That complicated his healing process.

Jimmy's life didn't turn out the way he expected it to. His depression became so severe he wasn't able to work. Now he's living in Baton Rouge again, his hometown. He seems to be happy and at peace. What more can you want for someone you love? Jimmy is like Peter Pan: in middle age, he still looks young. In some ways, he hasn't changed at all. He's still gentle, soft-spoken, and funny.

"I'm sorry, Jimmy," I said, the last time I saw him.

"For what?" he asked.

"For everything. For my selfishness. For the mean things I said, for the nice things I didn't say."

"We've had this conversation before," Jimmy said. "I've told you I forgive you, and you've said you forgive me. Do you think we can ever have a conversation that doesn't begin with apologies? The past is over."

Jimmy called a few months ago, and we talked about old times. I managed to keep myself from apologizing.

"Do you ever see Joe?" I asked.

Jimmy was silent. "Didn't you hear? He died in prison."

Sometimes when we talk, our conversation sounds like two old soldiers who have been through a war together. I was lucky, blessed to have Jimmy as long as I did. He loved me when I thought no one would. For that I am profoundly grateful.

Gray Eagle

Sometimes I've longed just to have someone hold me. A psychologist might say that desire represents a regression to infancy. Maybe so; it could also be that touch is free from the complicated issues of intimacy and AIDS. It's a need you never get over. I remember a time when I camped high in the mountains of New Mexico. My friend Ray and I lay out and looked at the stars. On clear nights when I can see Orion's belt I remember being held by Ray and feeling safe, comforted.

I went to high school with Ray; he was good-looking, tall with blond, curly hair. Five or six years after high school, I ran into him at the community center in Albuquerque and we started talking. We went for coffee and renewed our friendship, laughing at the memories of awkward adolescence.

Ray and I decided to go camping one weekend and spent a couple of crisp summer nights in the mountains. Ray held me like I wanted and needed; he put his arms around me and pulled me close. He told me he struggled with a drinking problem. He had looks, money, but no peace of mind. If anything good ever came from having AIDS, it helped make me empathetic with other people fighting physical or mental illness. It opened my eyes to the difficulties of others and the seriousness of addiction.

"All those stars out there, all of those worlds. Why are we here?" Ray whispered. "How did we get here?" he continued. "Where are we going?"

I said nothing, snuggling closer to him in the brisk night air.

"Just think," he mused. "We will never, never know." He sighed, not sadly. "No one knows. There aren't any answers. We'll never know."

When I was younger I might have insisted that some day we would know, that in the afterlife we would have answers. But I'd lost my certainty along the way and had too many questions.

Questions, those perplexing questions. Ray knew that there was no answer. Most times the answers don't matter, anyway: it's enough to be with friends, to love and care for others.

Often when I was distressed, the touch of a friend restored my tranquility.

My fondest experience of being held happened one cool, misty April night in Santa Fe. It was the night before Easter and there was a light rain.

I was supposed to meet a friend on the plaza. I walked along the covered sidewalks towards the center of town. It was mostly deserted; the drizzle kept people indoors. As I turned a corner, I came across a Native American man, the only person on the sidewalk. He was older, perhaps in his forties, bundled in a large, brightly-colored serape. We smiled at each other, perhaps sensing a mutual kinship that transcended age and ethnicity.

"It is cold tonight," he said softly, with the hint of a Pueblo accent.

I nodded.

"I am Gray Eagle. Walk with me a while." He was carrying a small sack of groceries.

"I'm meeting a friend," I explained. Gray Eagle smiled and took my hand. He held my chilly fingers tightly. I felt safe with him, like we were old friends from some past life.

We walked down the dark streets, speaking little. He smiled at me occasionally. Finally we came to the plaza, which was devoid of people.

"I will wait with you," he said. "Keep close to me."

We sat down on a bench. He pulled me towards him and wrapped his serape around us both. It was warm and comforting, protecting us from the drizzle of the cool night. Gray Eagle began to sing softly in his native tongue.

"I am singing a blessing for you," Gray Eagle said. "I am asking the spirits to watch over you, that you may always walk in beauty."

Peace came over me, a calm that I had not known for a long time. I felt like Gray Eagle understood and knew me, that he recognized my anxiety and discontent.

I looked up at the stars that were dimly shining through the misty mountain night. I remembered seeing the stars with Ray a couple of years earlier and his words echoed in my mind. "We will never know."

Maybe Ray was right. But sitting there, warm and safe in Gray Eagle's arms, it did not seem to matter. We would not know, we could never be sure about anything. Still, there were precious moments when, warm in someone's arms, all was well.

The Voice

I often felt sick in the afternoons. Usually after lunch my fever went up and my head ached. Fatigue sometimes forced me to bed. The mornings were all right, but in the afternoons I didn't feel well.

One afternoon was especially rough. I lay in the silence, watching the winter sun cast shadows on the wall. I could not drag myself out of bed. I looked at the clock, and promised myself to get up in an hour. I sighed, waiting for the nausea to subside, hoping to feel better. There was nothing to do but to wait. The idea of seeing friends cheered me: I knew that Jimmy and Joe would stop by at 5:00 p.m.

What was wrong, I wondered. Was it just the usual or was it something worse? I thought about making a doctor's appointment but that was often frustrating. Usually when I had some new symptom he would say, "We'll go ahead and run some tests but I suspect it's just the virus."

I was never satisfied with that answer. That afternoon I whispered out loud, "What is this?"

I lay there in the silent room and then asked, "Who is this?"

An inaudible voice answered. I didn't hear it as much as I felt it.

"I am death," was the answer. "I am near you."

Everything became clearer. I was clinging to life so fervently that I never listened to death. I did not want to hear him. But that afternoon I heard from my ever-present companion.

I knew death was not cruel or wicked. Death would prevail; death had come for some my friends and would eventually take us all.

A few years earlier I was jogging one summer morning. It was still: there was no wind, no cars driving by, and my racing mind calmed for a moment. The silence was audible and I was at peace. This was death, I remember thinking. Death was the stillness where nothing mattered. It was almost beautiful.

Though I was sad when friends died, there was occasionally a sense of relief, especially if they suffered a lot. Their pain was over; it's hard to see someone you love in discomfort and distress. Death ended all life's problems. Death would end my own pain and worry but it would also end my happiness.

The French say that death is like the sun; you can't look at it for too long. "It is hard to think about death," I overheard someone say one evening at a cocktail party.

"I don't think about it at all," another friend responded. "I figure by the time I get old, science will have figured something out."

It was a naïve statement, especially in those dark, early days of AIDS. The man who said those words died two years later.

I was aware of death that afternoon as I lay in bed. The sun began to sink lower in the sky till it was just an orange glow. I loved the sunset, the twilight time between day and night.

"You love the twilight because you are in the twilight of your life," my friend Donna once said.

Although I was just in my mid 20's, I worried that I was at the end of my existence. I fought it, though, and in the days before there was effective medicine, I tried every quack remedy and diet to combat my disease. People were trying scores of herbal cures and special food.

"I'm in the twilight years," my friend Sylvia once said. I had laughed at the time. Sylvia was a beautiful 45 year old who didn't think she was pretty. "Enjoy your youth," she advised.

Another friend once said that if he had known 16 was going to be middle-aged for him, he would have made a lot more out of those teenage years.

One lovely Southern spring day, my friend Cooper came to town. Cooper traveled a lot for his job, and sometimes when he drove through sleepy little Baton Rouge, he'd let me tag along on a road trip. That day I decided to skip class and tool around with him.

Cooper and I drove to St. Francisville, a picturesque little town that time and the Civil War had overlooked. We parked in front of a large old church near the center of town. Cooper and I got out and walked around the churchyard. The graves were very old: some of the tombstones were inscribed in French. The cemetery was shaded by live oak trees covered with Spanish moss. As we read the grave markers, I wondered about the lives of all those long-dead people. I hoped they had loved and that there had been friends who were sad to see them go.

Cemeteries are a good place to find serenity: my own relatives are buried in a shady pine-filled cemetery near a small town in Nebraska. It's a peaceful place and I will be lie there with my ancestors. I already have my tombstone.

Cooper was silent, and for a rare moment, so was I. He took my hand and finally spoke. "I feel like I have been missing something all these years," he said quietly. Cooper had grown up in the slums during the Depression; his life's goal was to be rich. He had succeeded but I suspected it had cost him. Maybe in pursuit of the material he'd overlooked the spiritual.

"There is something here," Cooper continued. "I don't believe in God..." his voice trailed off. Like him, I felt something in the cemetery, a presence. It was quiet, calm, eternal. In that graveyard I was overcome with sweet sadness. Maybe death had been with me all these years, my constant companion. I became aware of its presence in my quiet moments.

As I lay on my bed I thought about it. I remembered hearing that "still, small voice" as a child and thinking it was God. But whatever God was it didn't have an audible voice or tell you what to do. Today I can't say if my inner promptings come from God, my unconscious, or random neurons. Still, that still, small voice has guided me my whole life and I'm better off when I pay attention to it. I hear that voice when I practice inner silence.

Maybe the voice of death was my imagination. But I knew death held me with one hand while with the other I clenched the hand of life. Maybe they were the same thing; both hands of God.

In my mind's eye I pictured a Maypole, the kind I'd loved as a child. The ribbons are tied at the top and during the dance all the ribbons become entwined, one over the other. At the end the strings are woven around the pole. God is like the Maypole, I think: we are the ribbons entangled in the dance of life. We are part of God, part of death and life, God experiencing life through us, joined together at the end. The voice of God is the music that we dance to, the voice of life and death.

I lay there in the quiet, at peace. God, stillness, death. The phone rang, and I began to feel better. My friends were on their way, the strands of the Maypole were entwined.

The Party

I spent five years in the South working on a degree and I was finally finished. I'd been planning a party for over a year. Gaining the initials after my name wasn't what made me happy; rather, it was the fact that all my loved ones were going to be together. Though a number of friends had passed away, many were still with me. Harold, Jimmy, Joe, Carl and Martin, Peggy, Ruth, Bobbie, Pete and Millie: my friends covered the social spectrum from drag queens to nuns, and I invited them all to come. The guest list included religious friends, professors from the university, guys from my AIDS support group, and people from various political organizations. My family was coming to the party, too: my parents, grandparents, brother, my favorite cousin.

I made an effort to broaden my horizons in my early 20's. I'd come to realize that my bourgeois standards excluded many people from my life; arbitrary criteria kept me from seeing and experiencing things. When I opened my life up to people from various backgrounds my life became richer. My friends were my treasure. They were the reason I went on, we drew strength from each other. Everything in my life was subordinate to friendship: if I had to choose between money, career, and friends, there was no contest.

When I first came to Baton Rouge, I was looking for Mr. Right, my true love. In the process of growing up I learned to let go of that unrealistic dream. I felt so much love from my friends. "Lovers come and go," a friend once told me, "but you have your friends forever." Another friend said that friends are our real lovers. That special night, I knew it was true.

The party was held at a church hall. My friend Joe prepared a feast. In addition to running his family business, Joe was a chef. He made a buffet of Cajun dishes: there was gumbo, made with fresh shrimp from the nearby Gulf of Mexico; crawfish *etouffee* served with spicy Cajun rice; and quiche, which was *de rigueur* at any social gathering in the 1980's. Since the party was taking place at a church building alcohol was not served. That kept it from being a typical, south Louisiana party. Joe's friend Tim helped him in the kitchen.

The hall gradually filled with people. I looked around the room and saw the faces of the people I loved all through those Baton Rouge years. Were there friendships that lasted a lifetime? At that time I was too young to know. Once I read a thought-provoking article on the subject in the doctor's office. "Can a person have lifelong friends?" the author asked. I laughed when I turned the page: the end of the article was missing. I would never read if friendships could last a lifetime. That was something I would have to learn from experience.

People clustered in changing groups; I went from one to the next, saying hello, making sure everyone was having a good time. I overheard a lot of conversations. Pete and Millie had come up from New Orleans and were talking with Bobbie and my mother.

"I am sure it is your prayers that have kept your son alive," Bobbie said fervently to my mom. I knew how much Bobbie had prayed for her son Rick. She had masses said for him, recited the rosary, and made never-ending novenas for the health of her son. Why hadn't God heard her prayers?

My Jewish grandmother and her husband from the Midwest talked to Pete and Millie. My step-grandfather was a giant of a man, a life-long farmer. After their chat Pete whispered, "No wonder you're still alive. Look at the hearty grandfather of yours. You come from strong stock." My grandmother, on the other hand, was barely five feet tall. She's the one I take after in terms of height. My brother stood off by himself at first, perhaps uncomfortable around my gay friends. But as the evening wore on, he mingled more. He was trying. I saw Jimmy talk to him; Jimmy could talk to anyone. My favorite cousin had come all the way from California; she took off work to be there.

My professors came as well as a few friends from school. I wasn't as close as I might have been to my fellow students in the department. The university setting sometimes fosters adversarial, competitive relationships.

The academy knew I was gay. It was not something I chose to conceal. It's a misguided stereotype to think that colleges are liberal places, especially universities in the South. One professor felt compelled to psychoanalyze me: he told me I was only gay because there was a taboo against it. He explained that I had a secret fear of castration. I laughed.

I respected my professors and had much to learn from them. But I lived on my terms; one professor told me that I had too much of a social life. He said it would keep me from being a good scholar. I didn't care. I had this strange trump card, AIDS, which I felt gave me the right to spend my time as I pleased. Writing intellectual articles never made me as happy as hanging out with my friends.

Some of my worries were confirmed when I interviewed for teaching jobs. At a small college in Mississippi, I received an anonymous phone call the night before my interview with the dean. The caller warned me to come up with a girlfriend or fiancée; otherwise I wouldn't get the job. Sure enough, the dean asked me if I planned on getting married. I said no and wasn't offered the job. A college in Georgia that would have hired me wanted me to sign a moral contract saying I would uphold their church's teaching against gays.

There were gay professors, of course, and I knew many of them. Some came to my party. My friend Larry was there, who taught in another department. He was sick and died months afterwards. Martin had become ill by then; those of us with health problems knew each other. We were afraid of being fired or losing our medical insurance.

J.T. was there, along with some other clergy friends. J.T.'s presence meant so much to me; he was supportive and kind. He talked with Joe, the chef, and Tim, his assistant. Bobbie had joined them, and all three were being entertained by one of Joe's rollicking anecdotes. Tim seemed happy that night: seven days later, he shot himself. He was sick and was afraid he was going to die alone.

Death usually seemed like the enemy, the thing to be feared. But in moments of grief and suffering, it could seem like a welcome release. Some people congratulated me for being a "long-term survivor." But it's not always such a happy thing to outlive your buddies. I was always starting over, building a new network of friends when the old ones died.   As my life in Baton Rouge was ending I would start a new life somewhere   else.

I looked around the crowded room. Most of the people I loved were there. Still, I felt sad thinking of those who were absent. I missed Wayne, Rick and Beau; I felt a twinge of guilt remembering Alberto, who I had not even visited in the hospital. I thought of Dale and Pierre, the perfect couple. I tried not to wonder how many of my friends would be taken in the coming months and years. The future couldn't be known. It would unfold and we were helpless over fate.

Our lives were like a big party. AIDS was a nasty, loathsome guest who no one invited and who had no intentions of leaving. But it was still our party. We could choose to laugh, sing, and have fun. It was up to us to decide how to live. Happiness was a deliberate choice.

I wandered outside. For a moment I needed to be alone. Tears welled in my eyes; I wasn't sure if I was sad or happy. Bittersweet, I thought, it was bittersweet. Love heals AIDS, I had read somewhere. I felt so much love there that night. I didn't feel worthy. I wanted the moment to last even though I knew it could not.

I went back inside to the party. I remembered a religious class where everyone was given a ball of yarn. We were instructed to take the thread and give it to the people there we knew and loved. As we walked around the room we became entangled in a web of yarn. We formed a huge, chaotic tapestry.

I could have said that God had brought everyone in that party together. I didn't think that human connections occurred at random. But that warm Southern night, I decided to let the theologians worry about God. It was enough just loving people.

I would soon leave Baton Rouge with its wonderful people and my happy memories. I grew up and became a man in the South. In the following years, time I never expected to have, those experiences stayed with me. The friends I loved and those I lost remain a part of me. Knowing good people and having strong bonds of love prepared me for the years to come and gave me a base from which to grow.

For reasons I'll never know or understand I survived those early, difficult years of the epidemic. People much wiser and kinder than me did not.   Life isn't fair, like

Wayne always said. While nothing good can ever be said of AIDS, maybe it was a teacher, helping me to learn things I wouldn't have learned otherwise. Hopefully it gave me empathy for the suffering of others. I'm grateful for the gift of life and want to preserve the memory of those dear ones who have passed.